PRAISE FOR TED WRIGHT AND *FIZZ*

"Ted is a deeply intellectual poet laureate, who possesses an eclectic rare mix of right brain and left brain skills. He knows derivatives and da Vinci; and moves back and forth across these two parallel universes with inspiring ease. This modern-day Renaissance man is our planet's foremost thought leader on word of mouth strategy, and *Fizz* is the bible in this area. In an extremely thoughtful and engaging narrative, Ted takes a complex topic and boils it down into something extremely useful. If you want to truly understand how to harness the power of people talking, this book better head up your must-have reading list!"

    —DR. AMERICUS REED II, Whitney M. Young Jr. Professor of Marketing
                    at the Wharton School of the University of Pennsylvania

"If you want field-tested advice on how to inspire people to *love* and *talk* about what you do, this is the rare word of mouth marketing book that is actually worth talking about."

    —ROHIT BHARGAVA, bestselling author of *Likeonomics*

"It's more trusted. It's more authentic. It invades nobody's privacy. It's cheap as dirt. And, alone among the marketing arts, it is intrinsically human. Word of mouth would be the dominant category of marketing if only it could be harnessed. The thing is, as Ted Wright reveals in this charming primer, WOMM can be harnessed. In fact, it's happening right here and right now."

    —BOB GARFIELD, cohost of NPR's *On the Media*
                    and former columnist of *AdvertisingAge*

"Much has been written and probably much more has been said about how marketers can go about harnessing the power of word of mouth and brand advocacy to meet their objectives. With this book, Ted gives us valuable insights into why influencers play such an important role, who they are, and how they can be identified, and what the fundamental building blocks are for successful word of mouth efforts. By laying out these steps in the context of the various personal and professional experiences he has had, Ted lives up to one of the key factors he emphasizes as being critical for advocacy—the need for authenticity."

—PRADEEP K. CHINTAGUNTA, Joseph T. and Bernice S. Lewis
Distinguished Service Professor of Marketing at the
University of Chicago Booth School of Business

"I have always recommended a word of mouth approach to selling. Ted Wright has gone further and put a wonderful framework on this idea. Reading *Fizz* is like listening to a fascinating conversationalist share his life stories."

—PHILIP KOTLER, S. C. Johnson & Son
Distinguished Professor of International Marketing at the
Kellogg School of Management of Northwestern University

"I wish Ted had written this book before I started my career. His book is a TRU testament to the power of word of mouth marketing and the strategies that I embody every day."

—2CHAINZ, rap impresario and multiple Grammy Award nominee

"In a time of information overload, general advertising often turns people off. *Fizz* stresses the importance of identifying subcultures and developing approaches relevant for each. It emphasizes being creative in finding ways to get your message to your target audience. *Fizz* is filled with solutions."

—LYNETTE WRIGHT, Professor of Nursing (ret.) at Emory University

fizz

HARNESS THE POWER OF WORD OF MOUTH MARKETING
TO DRIVE BRAND GROWTH

TED WRIGHT

NEW YORK   CHICAGO   SAN FRANCISCO
ATHENS   LONDON   MADRID
MEXICO CITY   MILAN   NEW DELHI
SINGAPORE   SYDNEY   TORONTO

1 2 3 4 5 6 7 8 9 0 DOC/DOC 1 2 0 9 8 7 6 5 4

ISBN 978-0-07-183574-9
MHID   0-07-183574-1

e-ISBN 978-0-07-183575-6
e-MHID   0-07-183575-X

Cover design by Brandon Bennett
Interior design by Mauna Eichner and Lee Fukui

Library of Congress Cataloging-in-Publication Data

Wright, Ted.
 Fizz : harness the power of word of mouth marketing to drive brand growth / by Ted Wright.
    pages cm
 ISBN 978-0-07-183574-9 (alk. paper) — ISBN 0-07-183574-1 (alk. paper)
 1. Communication in marketing. 2. Branding (Marketing) I. Title.
 HF5415.1255W75 2015
 658.8'72—dc23
                                          2014027540

McGraw-Hill Education books are available at special quantity discounts to use as premiums and sales promotions or for use in corporate training programs. To contact a representative, please visit the Contact Us pages at www.mhprofessional.com.

To my wife, without whom I would be nothing. We have been together since 1987, and she has had my back since day one. She is the reason this book was written. I recognize that she is both smarter and nicer than I, so when she said, "You should really write a book," I heard her. My love for her knows no limit, and it's worth every effort in writing this book to be able to tell the whole world about her. If you ever see us together, make sure you talk to her first because she's the talent. I'm just lucky.

Contents

Acknowledgments

There are so many people to thank: teachers, including Mrs. Pullin and Steve Jaquier; Professors Heineman, Simms, Marion, Hawking, Schrager, McGill, Davis, and Zmijewski; and my friends Todd, Susan, Brawner, Toliver, and Joe.

Thanks to all the current and alumni employees of Fizz—with particular note to Judi, Tyson, Vanessa, Ross, and Tanya—all of whom have been vital to the growth of our firm. Further thanks also to my son, Abbott, who inspires me every day. A more creative and giving person does not exist.

Critically important to the creation of this book was Douglas Quenqua, without whom it would not have been written. Thank you to my editor, Casey Ebro, who worked tirelessly to make this book a success. Thank you also to everyone who read excerpts from the book, gave feedback, and otherwise spent their time to make sure it was as good as it could be.

Lastly, a shout-out to my mother and father, who had the grace to raise a son who was always asking questions and the fortitude to let me pursue my own path. Two better parents a man could not ask for.

Introduction

As I walked into the University of Chicago computer lab one early morning in 1999, I was greeted by the familiar sight of row upon row of blue-faced students. In those days, the reigning search engine was Netscape, and the Netscape screen reflected on their faces as an eerie cerulean glow. I put down my backpack and grabbed a terminal, taking my place among the blue faces.

It was my first year of business school. Netscape, for my purposes at the time, was adequate, if a bit frustrating. It was not the only game in town; AskJeeves, AltaVista, and Yahoo! already existed. But Netscape performed best on my standard search engine test, which was to enter my mother's name. As a renowned geneticist who shared a last name with other famous Wrights, my mother made a good digital shibboleth. If I entered "Lynette Wright," how many hits for the Wright Brothers or Frank Lloyd Wright would I have to sift through before finding one of my mother's papers? With Netscape, it was usually about seven or eight pages. Awful by today's standards, but not bad at the time.

On this particular day, Netscape was giving me trouble, enough to make me visibly upset, because the guy sitting to my left leaned over and offered some advice. "Have you thought about using Google?"

I had heard that word before, but only as a math term.

"It's a website," my new friend explained.

I typed in the website address, entered "Lynette Wright" in the search field, and for the first time ever, my mother's name was not only on the first page of the results but it was also the second hit overall. I had found my new search engine.

I thanked the guy and went back to work. Sure enough, 15 minutes later, the student to my right began cursing his computer. Eager to share my newfound knowledge, I leaned over and told him about Google. He, too, seemed grateful. By the time I stood up to leave, every blue face in the room had turned white. The glow of Netscape's blue screen had been replaced by Google's clean, white one. Word about the superior product had passed from person to person so quickly, yet so imperceptibly, that the room itself had been silently transformed.

I knew I had just witnessed something powerful, although I wasn't entirely sure what it was. I might never have thought about it again had something similar not happened a few weeks later.

Business school students generally don't watch a lot of television. Between classes and exams, who has time? But one day I heard about a magical product that automatically recorded TV shows without having to be reprogrammed every week. It could even pause live TV! Within weeks, everyone was talking about TiVo, and quite a few people owned a box of their own. My classmates started watching TV again.

What did TiVo and Google have in common? Yes, they inspired viruslike conversation among students, and that conversation led to widespread adoption. But it was more than that. It took me some time to put my finger on it. But once I did, it was a classic lightbulb-over-the-head moment.

There had been no advertising. These two products took over my campus with Ebola-like efficiency without the aid of a single ad.

Fascinating, I thought. I needed to know more.

I began researching what, at the time, I called "influencer marketing." Is it possible, I wondered, to forgo traditional advertising and instead use conversation between consumers to market a product? Could one actually harness the power of peer-to-peer conversation to advertise a brand? I learned that the idea was not a new one—it had been an art form for at least 3,000 years—but that nobody was thinking much about it in 1999.

I devoted my second year of business school to devising a set of questions and processes that would reveal what was "talkable" about any brand or product, and who was most likely to do the talking. By the time I graduated, I had designed what today would be considered an algorithm for influencer marketing. Over the years, my team and I have sharpened and refined this algorithm, coming up with better and smarter questions to elicit more useful answers. In the coming pages, I will go through these one by one, so you, too, can start using word of mouth to your advantage.

I started my firm soon after business school. For the past 13 years, I have been adding to my team and growing the business, now known as Fizz, into the global leader in word of mouth marketing. If you've ordered a Pabst Blue Ribbon, ridden an Italian scooter in Asia, bought a 4G LTE device, used chocolate milk to recover after a tough workout, cleaned your carpets with a Bissell sweeper, or bought numerous other products because of a friend's recommendation over the past 13 years, then you may have been touched by our work at Fizz.

But my education was hardly complete after leaving business school. In fact, just a few months after starting Fizz, I got the lesson of a lifetime when I took a full-time job with Delta Airlines. My goal was no less than to revolutionize Delta's marketing during business hours and build Fizz into a global powerhouse in my spare time.

Five months after I started at Delta, I earned a companywide award for innovation.

One month after that, I was fired.

Around the time I joined the company, Delta was under heavy attack from AirTran Airways. The young, upstart airline was siphoning away Delta's customers with cheap seats and a fun, irreverent attitude. Worse, AirTran was doing this in Atlanta, Delta's backyard (and my hometown).

Delta desperately needed a way to compete with AirTran. Unfortunately, promises of better food, more flights, added routes, or discounted seats wouldn't have done much good against a young nimble competitor like AirTran, which could afford to match us move for move. What could a longstanding legacy airline such as Delta offer customers that AirTran couldn't?

Maybe, I thought, Delta could turn its size and deep local roots into an advantage. After all, just as all Detroit residents know someone who works at Ford or General Motors, everyone who lives in Atlanta knows at least one Delta worker. I did some research and found that Delta employed more than 15,000 people locally. Using public records and some nimble math, I mapped employees by Zip code, revealing just how well dispersed Delta employees were throughout the city. It became clear that it was all but impossible to live in Atlanta without going to church, soccer games, PTA meetings, or the gym with at least one Delta employee. This was an advantage that the much smaller and younger AirTran definitely did not have.

What if we could use that to change the conversation? What if, I wondered, when Atlanta residents went to purchase a flight, they thought not about how much money they could save themselves but about the potential harm they were doing to their neighbors by opting for the slightly cheaper option? What if we could equate flying AirTran with taking food off your neighbor's table?

I wanted to make yard signs that every Delta employee in Atlanta could place outside his or her home. "Your Delta Neighbor Thanks You for Flying with Us" they would read. Not a guilt trip or even a plea. Just a simple thank you to humanize the company.

Not everyone loved the idea. "What if people start complaining to their neighbors about lost luggage?" nervous executives asked. "What if someone decides to bash in my mailbox because he didn't get enough peanuts?" My boss thanked me for the idea and swiftly dismissed it.

But I understood something the naysayers didn't. In word of mouth marketing, you always assume your audience is smart, at least as smart as you. Rather than talk to the lowest common denominator, or assume the worst in your audience, word of mouth marketing allows for—nay, depends on—the possibility that consumers are intelligent, rational, and able to make their own decisions based on the information you provide. The idea that a disgruntled customer would vent her frustration on a neighbor's mailbox because he was a phone operator for Delta just didn't seem rational to me. In reality, that's not how people behave.

So I went to Kinko's and printed up a sign—"This Delta Employee Thanks You for Flying with Us"—and stuck it on my front lawn, which faces a busy street. Worst-case scenario, I thought, I would be the victim of some drive-by heckling, after which I would take down the sign and admit I was wrong.

A few days after I put up the sign, my wife came home and asked why people kept honking and waving at our house. "Do you think it's the sign?" she asked. The next Saturday, I spent several hours sitting on our porch, which faced the street. Sure enough, quite a few drivers would honk or wave when they saw the sign. Over the next eight weeks, I had five people stop at my house because of the sign. Four were Delta employees who wanted to know how they could get one. The other was a customer who wanted to share a story of how Delta employees helped carry her son on a plane after he had broken his leg. Not one was angrily looking for his lost luggage.

I went back to my boss and told her about my experiment. Unfortunately, she was not in the habit of saying yes after she had said no. She shot me down again. Hard.

This is the point in the story when a more rational person would admit defeat. But I will tell you, dear reader, that I am not a more rational person—not when it comes to Atlanta. You see, it's where I'm from, it's where my parents are from, and it's where their parents are from. Atlanta's success is very important to me on a personal level. I want the Falcons to always win, I want Delta to always be on time, I want Coca-Cola to sell more stuff than Pepsi does. That's just who I am.

So instead of letting it go, I took the sign from my yard and taped it to my office door. The same door that I knew the Delta CMO walked past at least once a day. To be sure, it was a brash, risky move, particularly for a 30-year-old brand manager. But such was my faith in my idea that I truly believed it would inspire others to overlook my insouciance.

Before long, someone who reported directly to my CMO—that would be my boss's boss—knocked on my office door. "Can you tell me about the sign?" she said.

I told her about my home experiment and the reaction I had gotten. Then I pulled out the map I'd made of all Delta employees in Atlanta. But by this point, I had added much more information to it. I had overlaid segmentation data, such as voter registration figures and demographic stats. She looked at me half-amazed, half-perplexed, thanked me, and left the office.

At the next weekly staff meeting, I was given an award for innovation. And at the next big all-employee rally, the company handed out signs like the one I had made. Naturally, people loved them because there is, and always has been, a lot of pride in being a Delta employee. People hugged me; some asked if they could get extra signs for their friends who used to work for Delta. I felt triumphant.

Five weeks later I was fired for insubordination.

Frankly, I don't blame anyone but myself. What I did was out of line and potentially embarrassing to my boss and others. But as with so many things in life, it turned out to be the best thing that could have happened to me. From that moment on, I focused 100 percent of my energies on Fizz, and it has gotten us where we are today.

We at Fizz truly believe we are on to something. Heck, I thought we were on to something 13 years ago. When you have a moment, go to our website and check out our mission statement. I know, I know, could anything be more boring? Trust me when I tell you this mission statement is . . . different. And certainly not boring. Hint: It's NSFW.

Having a killer team, living on the cutting edge, being rebellious, being right—these are the things that bring me joy. Thus Fizz was created and has grown along the path it has taken. Maybe you agree with that philosophy. At the very least, you'll agree with the success we've garnered for our clients, the kind of success you can't get through TV commercials, print ads, or billboards. At least not anymore.

Word of mouth marketing has always existed. We've just found a better and more efficient way to do it by using a method that is both replicable and remarkably consistent. My hope is to share some of those secrets with you and help you get started on your own word of mouth program. Maybe you'll decide word of mouth marketing is for you; maybe you won't. Either way, I promise you'll walk away with a better understanding of how consumers today are driven by conversation—and how that can help you sell more stuff to more people more often for more money.

CHAPTER 1

Influencers: Who They Are and Why You Need Them

CASE STUDY: PABST BLUE RIBBON

Pabst Blue Ribbon (PBR) was dead.

It was 2001, and the iconic American brew was on track to sell fewer than a million barrels of beer in the United States for the year, capping 23 straight years of declining sales.[1] To put that in perspective, PBR had regularly sold more than 20 million barrels a year to U.S. consumers in the 1970s.[2] But by 2001, the brand had sunk so low that there was little to no hope of resuscitation.

It was around then that my team and I got the call to help bring it back. But there was a catch: there would be no advertising and no traditional marketing of any kind. And our marketing budget would be only slightly more than zero. To be honest, my firm got the job largely because we were young, brash, and cheap. I couldn't have been more proud.

How did PBR achieve this lowly state? Partially by design. In 1985, Paul Kalmanovitz, a brewing and real estate magnate, assumed control of Pabst Brewing Company, which included brands like Lone Star and Olympia. Some believe that Kalmanovitz intentionally neglected the PBR brand so that its somewhat tarnished, blue-collar image would fade from public view, at which point he could build it back up again from scratch. For years, PBR received virtually no advertising or promotional support.

The first part of Kalmanovitz's plan worked beautifully. Unfortunately, he died before he had a chance to initiate phase 2. And he made an even bigger mistake: Kalmanovitz left the brand to a charitable trust, violating a U.S. law that prohibits charities from owning for-profit companies. Ultimately, the IRS gave the trust until 2010 to sell the business.[3]

Neal Stewart, PBR's brand manager, came to me for help. Together, we scoured the company's sales data, looking for any sign of hope, some spark we could fan into a flame. Soon, we noticed something intriguing. There were five places in America that PBR was selling, all with seemingly very different demographics. In these cities, sales were not only healthy (relatively speaking) but growing. Neal and I scratched our heads trying to figure out what it was about those cities. We hopped on a plane and checked out as many as our meager funds would allow, thereby expending most of our marketing budget.

As we talked with PBR drinkers, a picture began to emerge. Many of these new customers had just turned 21, meaning they had been born in the late 1970s. A lot of these young people had hardcore yuppies for parents.

Today, the term *yuppie* refers to any moderately ambitious young person with a good job, a nice apartment, and no visible tattoos. But when they first emerged in the late 1970s and early 1980s, yuppies were a kind of political movement of people who strongly rejected the 1960s counterculture. They were anti-hippies who embraced structure, money, and status symbols like Polo shirts and "Beamers."

In order to rebel against their yuppie parents, these young people had decided to buy their clothes from the Salvation Army, work as bike messengers or tattoo artists, grow ridiculous side-burns, and drink the least pretentious, most unglamorous beers they could find.

These were the early hipsters. Like *yuppie*, the meaning of *hipster* has now been watered down to mean anyone with skinny jeans and a pack of American Spirit. But back then, hipsters were building a new ethos for their generation, one that rejected tradi-tional notions of status and prestige. The more a thing was con-sidered "cool" by the mainstream, the less these young people wanted to do with it. The worst transgression for a hipster was to do something just because he wanted to be seen doing it, whether it was drinking a particular brand of beer or driving a particular kind of car. The key word was *authentic*. So they swarmed to things that the mainstream culture deemed hopelessly unhip.

At the time, nothing was less hip than PBR. Nothing was cheaper either. And the newly perceived target market was highly price sensitive.

The fact that PBR had no money for traditional advertising was a blessing in disguise. Throwing a bunch of TV commercials on the air, particularly ones that tried to capitalize on the brand's newfound hipster cred, would have been a disaster. The fact that these young people had never seen a PBR ad was a huge selling point for them. It reminded them of a time when men drank beer because they liked to, not because they had been promised a backyard full of bikini models. Traditional advertising, particularly of the kind produced by big beer companies in those days, would have killed whatever tiny momentum the brand had built. In fact, any indication that the brand was trying too hard to be liked would have backfired big time.

Not that I was a fan of traditional advertising anyway. Even as a relatively young person in 2001, I had seen the writing on the wall. Broadcast wasn't working the way it used to, and the big success stories of the day, brands such as Google and TiVo, were thriving due to word of mouth, not TV commercials. The trick was to get the most influential people among this already influential group of early hipsters to talk to their friends about PBR. All we had to do was give them good stories to share.

First, Neal and I figured out what made the brand *talkable* (a word you'll be seeing a lot in this book). By talking to the young people in Portland and Pittsburgh, we discovered that they loved PBR for being unpretentious and low profile. So we hit the streets and started offering our support to creative people doing cool, interesting things just for the sake of it. If we found young people having bike messenger races, we'd hang out with them and offer them a sign to hang at their next event. We brought beer and hats to gallery openings, skating parties, juggling contests—you name it. We gave six packs of beer to Mini Kiss, a Kiss tribute band whose members were all little people.

And we never just handed out stuff and walked away. We talked to these young people about the stuff they were into. And of course, we talked about the beer.

There were no scantily clad girls passing out glow-in-the-dark coasters in sports bars, and there were no brand executives in suits making sure the events didn't violate their corporate guidelines. If we gave someone a sign, he wasn't required to hang it a certain way or to guarantee a certain number of attendees.

The message was simple: PBR thinks you're awesome, and we want to help you keep being awesome.

For someone who isn't looking to be recognized, recognition—particularly from a beloved brand—can be a powerful thing. Even more powerful is when that brand asks for nothing in return. We made an impression with these young people, and we started a lot of conversations.

Slowly but surely, the brand began to grow (Figure 1.1). As the new hipster "tribe" spread out across the country, they brought a

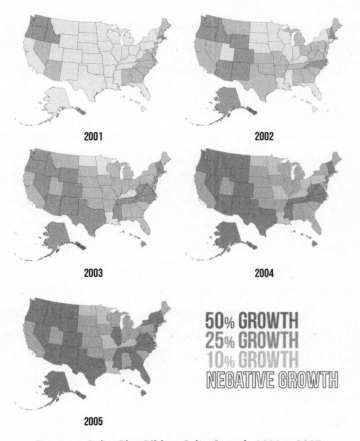

Figure 1.1 **Pabst Blue Ribbon Sales Growth, 2001 to 2005**

love of PBR with them. It required a lot of legwork from Neal, the brand, me, and a lot of others, but PBR gradually became the cool beer to drink if you didn't care about being cool.

In 2002, PBR grew 5 percent. In 2003 and 2004, it grew 15 percent. In 2004, Pabst Brewing Company was featured in a *New York Times Magazine* story with the headline "The Marketing of No Marketing," and it was named one of *Fast Company*'s Most Innovative Companies.[4]

By 2006, PBR had recorded a combined annual growth of 55 percent, and it had almost doubled its volume. Whereas in 2001 PBR was showing no growth in all but 14 U.S. states, by 2006 it had grown a minimum of 10 percent in every state, and 50 percent in more than 30 states.[5] From 2008 to 2012, it was one of the top-growing beer brands in the United States.

The program worked because we gave influential people a great story to share: the story of an honest, unpretentious beer brand that genuinely supports individualism and creativity. Today, PBR is as closely associated with hipsters as Arcade Fire and ironic facial hair. So much so that, at this point, the company can sit back and reap the rewards of the consumer-to-consumer brand advocacy that results from word of mouth marketing.

All vital brands have a story to tell. Every story will be relevant and interesting to some group of people out there. And among every group of people are the *influencers*: the 10 percent who are compelled by their nature to tell friends about this cool new thing they found.

People are talking, and brands are a big part of the conversation. You just have to give them something to talk about.

Writers have to write, singers have to sing, and influencers have to share stories with their friends.

It really is that simple. Influencers—a group that we now know makes up about 10 percent of the population across all ages—are compelled to talk about their passions to friends, family members, and even strangers who share their interests. It is a psychological necessity for them. Just as Michael Stipe would probably go mad without producing some kind of art, or Stephen King would wither and die without his typewriter, influencers would feel pain if they couldn't share their stories with people.

What happens to a person in childhood to generate this personality trait? Who knows? Frankly, who cares? The point is, these people exist, and you cannot stop them from sharing stories.

What you can do is get them to spread stories about your brand or product. You just have to hand the right story to the right people at the right time. Or as I like to say, if you want to catch fish, you have to use the proper bait. The trick is coming up with the best bait possible and throwing it to the fish you want to catch.

This is how word of mouth marketing works. And it does work, far better than any other form of marketing does these days. You just have to learn how to fish. This book will teach you how to do that.

THE RISE OF THE INFLUENCERS

Influencers are the key to word of mouth marketing. They are the ones who will carry the story about your brand or product from person to person.

If you are in marketing, you have known about influencers for a long time now. Still, it's remarkable how little most of us really *know* about them. If you're going to conduct word of mouth marketing, you need to understand what makes influencers do their thing, and how it affects other people.

Though influencers have always existed, it has only been in the last 25 years that marketers have needed to concern themselves with them. Prior to that, mainstream media did a great job helping the cereal makers and gas stations and movie studios of the world sell stuff. For every dollar they spent on TV ads, they knew they could expect more than a dollar in return. So everyone bought as much commercial time as they could. A full-page ad in the local paper got your small business a lot of attention and started conversations. Influence was something you could buy by the inch or by the second.

In the mid-1990s, as technologies and tastes began to evolve, those returns started to diminish. Some marketers saw the writing on the wall; others tried to wait it out. Today, many of the channels that used to work have become utterly ineffective. Others don't even exist anymore. How many towns in America even have a daily newspaper these days? The old ways of doing business are gone, and marketers are searching for another way.

In a deeply fragmented culture such as ours, where people have tuned out advertising and tuned in to their own deeply individualized communities, no single channel is as consistent, effective, or reliable as those maintained by real influencers.

A Brief History of Influencer Research

How do we know that influencers are real? Our first hint came in 1940, when sociologist Paul Felix Lazarsfeld conducted his now-legendary "People's Choice" study. During the 1940 presidential election season, Lazarsfeld and his colleagues repeatedly interviewed thousands of voters to track how they decided which candidate to support. Their study divided voters into two groups:

"opinion leaders" and "opinion followers." The latter group made its decisions based largely on information passed on to them by the former, much smaller group.

Since then, decades of market research have shown that this dynamic holds true in all realms of life, not just politics. Decisions about what to buy, what trends to follow, even where to live, all hinge largely on the power of the few most influential people among us.

In his 1984 book, *Influence: the Psychology of Persuasion*, Robert Cialdini identified the six key principles of influence: reciprocity, commitment and consistency, social proof, authority, liking, and scarcity. His book is required reading for anyone who needs to understand the dynamics of influence.

In his 2003 book, *The Influentials*, word of mouth marketing pioneer Ed Keller told us who the influencers were and how many of them were out there. Through extensive research, he had found that 1 in 10 Americans was making most of the buying decisions for the other 9. That 10 percent was responsible for everything from the shift toward energy-efficient cars in the 1970s to the mass adoption of cell phones in the 2000s, he wrote. And as the culture became ever more fragmented, he said, that 10 percent only became more powerful.

Now, I'm going to tell you how to find influencers and make them work for you.

What Are Influencers?

Influencers are not necessarily the most affluent people, nor the best educated. They are not, as people often assume, the vaunted "early adopters" so worshipped in our tech-obsessed culture.

Influencers are the people most deeply involved in their community, however that community is defined. It can be a school district, a college fraternity, a sub-Reddit devoted to chemistry, or a group of Portland hipsters. They are the ones constantly sharing their thoughts on the latest trend, article, or product that they know interests you too. They are the ones who told you about the latest restaurant you tried or who warned you about that awful movie you nearly saw. They are the ones who always seem to know about the trends before you do.

Having studied, thought about, and worked with them over the course of my career, I have observed that all influencers share three personality traits. Let's take a look at each one.

They Are Compelled to Share Stories with Friends

In the movie *City Slickers*, the Daniel Stern character says he talked to his dad about baseball as a teenager because they couldn't talk about anything else. It's the only way they were able to express their love for each other.

For influencers, sharing stories is an expression of love. It is how they build and deepen relationships with people. They can't just walk around all day saying, "I would like to have a closer relationship with you." Instead, they share stories to build ties with the people around them.

Because they have this compulsion, influencers have arranged their lives to collect information about the things they're passionate about. After all, they need to feed the beast. They know what they are interested in, and they are sure to find out about it first. They always want to bring you new information.

They Like to Try New Things Because They're New

Lots of us like to try new things. But not all of us want to try new things simply because they are new. This is what makes influencers special. They don't need incentives or persuasion. For them, newness is a selling point all its own.

Think about it: influencers need stories to share with people, and what's easier to talk about than, "I tried this new thing you will love"? Stories about new things provide fresh content for influencers, so they are always in search of them.

A middle-aged golf enthusiast will drive three towns over to be the first to try the buzzed-about new putter. A twentysomething influencer will go out on a rainy Monday night to hear a new band before her friends do. A 10-year-old influencer will subscribe to the Lego catalog so that he can tell his friends about the new play sets before they hit stores.

An influencer knows if he has information first, you will not only listen to what he says but you will also come back to him for another conversation once you have something to say about it. Yay, more conversation! He also knows that if he has tried something many more times than you have, you will come to regard him as an expert, and you will seek his counsel when you have questions on the topic.

New information is fuel for influencers, so they are drawn to things that they haven't heard of before. You don't have to worry about incentivizing influencers to sample that new toothpaste or listen to that new recording. The incentive is already there. Just say the word "new."

PRO TIP

"New" doesn't always have to be 100 percent new.

Sometimes, a new idea is simply an old one placed in a new context. Consider one of the programs Fizz ran for BISSELL sweepers—a product that technically hasn't been new for a while.

In 2011, to place the sweepers in a new context for a new audience, we started bringing them to RV parks. Now, if you know anything about the RV community, you know that it includes a lot of retirees and that these folks almost always tend to have a pet dog or cat. That means a lot of fur and dirt in a very small space. These folks also usually have a lot of pride in the appearance of their RVs—when you've stopped for the night in a park or lot, you may want to invite some new friends over for a cocktail or a card game or just to show off your mobile home. The last thing you want in those cases is a dirty, fur-strewn RV. But space is precious in these vehicles, and few people have room for a full-size vacuum cleaner.

So we took some sweepers and drove around in a golf cart, offering to clean people's RVs for them. After some initial awkwardness, the RV owners usually let us in to perform a quick sweep—and to open their eyes to a whole new way of keeping their campers clean.

Surely, they had all heard of BISSELL sweepers before. But it wasn't until they saw us cleaning their campers in five minutes or less that they realized what a natural fit the product would be for their lifestyle. Because it made so much sense, the idea caught on quickly once it was introduced.

Three months into this program, we were getting calls from national RV jamborees with 15,000 coaches asking us to show up in our golf carts with sweepers. Nine months in, we had RV manufacturers asking us to set up near their displays at these jamborees because they thought it would bring them more foot traffic. Though this was far from the only program we ran for BISSELL (you'll hear more about them later), the company's sweeper sales increased 45 percent by 2013.

BISSELL sweepers quickly became a must-have RV accessory—not because they were new but because the idea was new.

They Are Intrinsically Motivated

True influencers are compelled by something deep inside them to share stories about brands and products. It's just the way they are.

Trying to motivate them through discounts or rebates won't work. In fact, most influencers will be driven away by such things because they will feel that you're trying to buy their loyalty rather than earn it. Worse, your financial incentive might pollute the relationships they are trying to build by telling stories about your brand.

Let me explain with an example from my own work.

A few years ago, my agency was helping out a private school called Academe of the Oaks in our hometown of Atlanta, Georgia. This school overwhelmingly relied on word of mouth from its students' parents to bring in new applicants. To drive that word of mouth, the school offered a $500 tuition rebate to any parent who referred a new family. Basically, the school was betting that at least some of its students' parents were community influencers.

To keep track of the referrals, the school asked new families to write the name of the person who referred them at the bottom of the application.

Big mistake.

In three years of running this program, only a few parents claimed their tuition discount. Why? Because the program was a turnoff to parents who actually had influencer personalities. The last thing they wanted was their friends' thinking that they were recommending the school just to get $500 off their own tuition. The program was killing word of mouth because it provided exactly the wrong kind of motivation for influencers.

By convincing them to drop the $500 bounty and to use a few other word of mouth tactics—which we'll discuss in Chapter 3— we moved the school from budget crisis to expansion mode. Now it has kids on waiting lists.

Influencers share stories because they want to build bonds with people. For them, that is the reward, and it comes from a place deep within them. If they think what you're selling will be interesting to people they know, that is all the motivation they need. You cannot buy their interest—or their approval—with discounts or rewards.

For dyed-in-the-wool marketers, people who have spent their entire careers trying to entice consumers with offers, this can be a tough mindset to grasp. I get that. We have been trained to dangle 10 percent off, two-for-one, limited-time-only promos. But those things won't work well with the influencers. So working with them means thinking differently.

The Rising Power of Influencers

The influencer ecosystem is very much a democracy. Power is granted by the people. The only reason influencers have any power at all is that 90 percent of the population willingly follows their lead. That 10 percent sets the trends, and the rest of us go along with them. Most of the time, we don't even realize it. But we are happy to do it.

This is true across every category and every age group. Middle-aged men are following influencers when they buy a BMW as much as seven-year-old girls are when they buy Silly Bandz (or, more accurately, pester their parents to). Regardless, the 10 percent rule holds: 10 percent of the population decides what to buy, the other 90 percent goes along for the ride.

Though influencers have probably always existed in some sense, they have never held more power than they do now. There are a couple of reasons for this.

PRO TIP

Not every influencer is obvious.

One time, I was looking to hire a Los Angeles market manager for Tiger beer. It would be this person's job to start conversations about Tiger beer in the local bar scene. We needed someone naturally influential in that community, so of course I was picturing someone who looked a little rock and roll. More Kurt Cobain than Britney Spears.

Because of that assumption, I almost didn't hire someone perfect for the job. *(continues)*

When we received this person's résumé, we didn't think too much of it. She was an assistant manager at a Target store, and she had no real beer or nightlife experience to speak of. But she did well on the phone interview, so we brought her in for a face-to-face meeting.

She pulled up in a big white Lexus and teetered in on four-inch stilettos, carrying what must have been a $1,000 handbag. I thought, "Well, this won't take long." She could not have looked any less the part.

To get her talking (it's always good to get your potential brand ambassadors talking), I asked her about the jeans she was wearing. Over the next seven minutes, she proceeded to give me a PhD-level discourse on what those jeans meant, where they came from, where they should be worn, where they shouldn't be worn, who is and isn't allowed to wear them, and so on. She was the Margaret Mead of denim in Southern California. So of course, that got me interested.

"Which bars do you think Tiger beer would be good in?" I asked.

"Do you mean the bars that are open now," she responded, "or the ones that will be open next week?" She then explained the entire ecosystem of Southern California nightlife to me: the people, the players, who's cool now, who isn't, who might be cool if they can get the right stuff. Clearly, she was part of this community, and I almost dismissed her because she didn't look the part.

Remember, get your potential influencers to communicate with you. Listen to them to find out who and what they know, and who might be listening to them. Maybe the woman in front of you doesn't have kids, but she might have nine nieces and nephews she's helped raise, and so she has a lot of influence among people buying gifts for toddlers. You never know until you talk to them because not every influencer is obvious.

Consumers Have Lost Faith

Everyday people have lost faith in mass media and, particularly, in marketing messages. According to a 2010 study by social scientist and marketing researcher Daniel Yankelovich, 75 percent of Americans do not believe that companies tell the truth in their advertising, and that's across all channels. So we bailed. We have been so inundated with jingles and promises and guarantees for so long that we have simply tuned them out (and thanks to technologies like DVRs and ad blockers, we can). From the mid-1990s to the mid-2000s, we gradually gave up on the idea that companies are going to help us make good decisions. These days, I expect my friends to help me do that, and so do most other people.

That is not an opinion. It is a fact—and a well-established one at that. According to a 2010 report by McKinsey & Company, up to 50 percent of all purchasing decisions are based primarily on a friend's recommendation. And according to research firm Nielsen, 92 percent of consumers trust recommendations from people they know, and—this is the most amazing part—70 percent trust online recommendations from strangers.[6]

Yes, they would rather trust a stranger on the Internet than your TV commercial.

The Culture Is Atomized

In the music business, it is largely accepted that the days of block-buster album sales—Michael Jackson's *Thriller*, U2's *Joshua Tree*, records that sell tens of millions of copies—are long behind us. This is because there is no single pop culture anymore. Today, we are all tuned in to our own subcultures, our own personalized media mixes. And each of these subcultures has its own influencer class. All the emo kids listen to a handful of emo influencers, all the marathon runners listen to the running influencers, and so on. Mass media simply isn't set up to address that kind of specialization.

Once in a while, an artist breaks into what remains of the mainstream to become a crossover hit, like Lady Gaga or Katy Perry. But even their albums rarely sell more than 2 or 3 million copies. *Thriller*, by comparison, has sold somewhere between 60 and 100 million.[7]

Influencers, on the other hand, thrive on it. Nothing thrills an influencer like having a group of people coming to her for advice and recommendations on a mutual obsession. In this way, a segmented culture reinforces its own divisions. For example, once I know that people look to me for guidance on, say, classic horror movies, I am going to double my efforts at becoming an expert in the field.

That is an enormous amount of buying power in the hands of a few people. These days, a word from a friend or an established expert in his category is far more powerful than any TV commercial starring a celebrity, no matter how much that celebrity may be getting paid.

The power of word of mouth marketing is that it is a targeted message from a trusted source, every single time.

Who Has Time?

Another reason we look to influencers more now is that we are simply too busy. Time and money are scarce. As an average American who is fully consumed with my job, my family, and all my other commitments, I do not have time to research what tequila I should be buying or what gym I should join. Frankly, these things aren't that important to me. Instead, I let my influencer friends— to whom these things *are* important—figure that out for me. Then, the one time every year that I need it, I call them and ask for their recommendation.

So why do companies still spend time trying to reach 100 percent of the population with their advertising messages?

Excellent question. In my experience, most marketers already know that there is a lot of waste when using this channel. They know that the vast majority of people who see their commercials will not be moved to do or buy anything, much less convince anyone else to. But as the classic John Wanamaker quote (which, because this is a marketing book, I am legally obligated to include) goes, most marketers know that half their advertising budget is being wasted, they just don't know which half. So they keep spending all of it in the hopes that some of it will make an impact.

The truth is, if you are spending most of your budget on media that promises reach and frequency (I'm looking at you, broadcast television), you are probably wasting far more than half of your advertising budget. Actually, 90 percent is more like it.

As those channels have broken down, influencer networks have strengthened. Luckily for us, that makes them easier than ever to find.

PRO TIP

Most of you will still be broadcasting in some form.

In my experience, if you can manage to work the theme of your word of mouth campaign into your broadcast work, you will end up supercharging both. It is hard to do, particularly if your company is trying word of mouth marketing only as a test. But if you can combine the two so that one reflects the other, both will become more powerful and resonate further.

When Broadcast Works: Axe Body Spray

Broadcast is not the wrong choice for every product. There are still some marketing campaigns for which broadcast is not only the smart choice but the only choice. Take, for example, Axe body spray.

Axe's essential message is: "Spray this stuff on your body, and supermodels will seemingly fall from the ceiling and writhe upon you." I don't think I'm spilling any secrets by saying this is not true. Still, if the playful sexism doesn't bother you, they are pretty good commercials. And given the stunning success of the product, pretty effective ones too.

Axe's message can exist only in broadcast. And it certainly wouldn't work as a word of mouth campaign. Imagine you're 15 years old and playing video games with your buddy when you turn to him and say, "Dude, there's this thing called Axe body spray, and if you use it, bikini-clad supermodels will literally chase you around the beach." Twenty-four hours later, that buddy will be standing at your door demanding his money back.

And yes, broadcast provides a timeliness that word of mouth clearly cannot. Pizza companies will always see a spike in orders when it runs an ad right before the Super Bowl. My friends in the business say they make the money back and then some, so they've found a profitable niche they will mine as long as they can. Clearly, there are some objectives broadcast can still help you achieve. There are simply much, much fewer of them than there used to be.

Just ask Quiznos, which relied primarily on ads and coupons for its marketing. It filed for Chapter 11 bankruptcy in March 2014. Now it's their company that's "toasty."

Party Trick

Tell enough marketers that traditional media has almost no chance of helping them sell stuff, and you will inevitably get lots of uncomfortable looks. Here's a little party game I like to play with these people.

I say to them: Pick a category of products sold in the United States. Automotive, technology, fast food, anything. Then, pick a time range: three years, five years, your choice. Finally, you tell me: Within that time period and within that category in the United States, how many campaigns do you think have been really effective at selling more stuff? How many moved the needle? Typically, their answer will be between three and six. In this scenario, we'll say four.

That's your numerator.

(continues)

Now, I say, tell me how many ad campaigns from that category you think took place overall. Depending on the category, it will usually be about 50. (In reality, it would almost always be higher, but remember, this is a party. Be nice.)

That's your denominator.

Then I tell them to simply do the math. Divide through, I say. The resulting number is the chances that their traditional media campaign will be successful. Behold: $4 \div 50 = 0.08$. That's an 8 percent chance of success.

At this point, it may be necessary to remind your new friends that these are numbers of their own choosing. But that probably won't be necessary, depending on the number of cocktails they've had.

If they are still not convinced, ask them to tell you about all the billboards between their house and their office. How many can they name? How many of the billboards' intended messages can your friends repeat to you? Because some company is out there paying for those signs on the basis that your friends are driving past them every day. Yet your friends cannot tell you what they say or what they are trying to sell. And guess what. Your friends are not any different from anybody else.

FINDING INFLUENCERS

When I think about influencers, I think about the first time I visited Hawaii. I remember looking out at the water and thinking how beautiful it was. I couldn't see any fish, and at least at first, I didn't really think about them. It was enough to appreciate what I could see of the ocean from a distance.

Then I decided to go snorkeling. Once I put my mask on and my head underwater, I discovered about 50 fish swimming around me. It was a whole other world, and it was gorgeous. Had I never put my head underwater, I never would have seen they were there. The fish didn't care either way.

Influencers are a lot like that. Most of the time, we don't think about them, largely because we can't see them. But they are out there, doing their thing, whether you pay attention to them or not. If you want to figure them out, you have to get your head below the surface.

There are three rules to finding and working with influencers: let them come to you, use the right bait, and fish where the fish are.

Rule 1. Let Them Come to You

If I gave you a net and fins and a speargun, could you catch a fish? Maybe. You would have to swim very fast and take careful aim at a moving target. But you might be able to do it. Of course, that would get you only one fish, and you would have expended an awful lot of time and energy.

Or you can let them come to you.

It's the same with influencers. There are plenty of agencies and research firms that would be thrilled to take your money to help you find the people who are most likely to be influential in your category. You can then bring those alleged influencers into your office and ask them questions about their passions and hobbies. Observe them. Are they sharing stories with you in a way that indicates they do so naturally? Do they seem to have good social skills? Do they show genuine enthusiasm about certain products or topics? You can go through all the checklists and say, "OK, this person may be an influencer."

But there is an easier and far more effective way to attract influencers. Get some good bait and dangle it in the water. The truly passionate people will come check it out. They will come to you. The trick is figuring out what bait to use for the particular fish you want to catch.

Rule 2. Use the Right Bait

Follow me back to Hawaii for a moment. As I was snorkeling, some guy, clearly a local, waded into the water carrying a bag of frozen peas—not your usual beach snack. Well, this guy knew what he was doing. He grabbed a handful of those peas and threw them in the water.

If I was impressed by the 50 fish I saw when I first put my head underwater, I was downright astonished at what the peas attracted: the 50 fish turned into about 300! And every kind you could imagine, just streaming out of the reef—which itself is stocked with nutrients—to check out the peas.

Just like the fish, influencers are swimming around in a sea of information, but they are always looking for new stories to consume. They love a good story, or an opportunity to share something new. You just have to offer them the right bait. That's how you lure an influencer.

In the case of marketers, your bait is a story about your brand or product. The trick is figuring out what the right story is and presenting it in a way that is most attractive to influencers.

You have to offer something of interest. Something authentic, new, interesting, and cool. In short, something worth talking about.

Let's start with a bad example of influencer bait. Let's say you are a furniture company, and you make a high chair that is so wonderfully designed it's been included on lists of the best-designed items on earth. You have a hugely devoted following, and most people with young children have at least heard of your chair. Now, here comes the seventy-fifth anniversary of your company, and you want to sing it from the mountaintops. Well, guess what? Other than your employees and another 20 fans worldwide who have named their children after your company, nobody cares. In fact, other than those people, nobody cares about any of the following: your anniversary, the fact that your company is family owned, or how proud you are that your grandfather started the company 75 years ago. Too many companies want to talk about stuff that matters greatly within their four walls but isn't likely to inspire a single conversation outside of them. Don't fall into the trap of thinking that just because it's important to you, it's interesting to anybody else.

Here's some good influencer bait: a new study shows that children who use your high chair sit in an adult chair and feed themselves far earlier than other kids. That's a story that will get picked up and talked about because it is relevant and interesting to parents of young children everywhere.

You need to ask yourself, what is something about my brand that can really inspire a conversation? And who are the people who will want to have this conversation?

It's important to note that not all the fish actually ate those peas. Some just swam up, tasted them, and then went about their fishy business. Others only glanced at them and swam past. Some, of course, gobbled them up.

Even if your brand story hits all the right notes, not every influencer is going to be interested in it. That's natural. No influencer is influential in every category. In fact, we find that most are influential in three to five categories maximum. So you need to make sure you're offering the right bait to the right fish.

Of course, you have to get the bait in front of the fish. Which brings us to our third rule.

PRO TIP

Fishermen will tell you that a bright, shiny object is sometimes your best bait.

The same is true in word of mouth marketing.

In 2009, Fizz was trying to start conversations about a decades-old soda brand known mostly in Southern California. This brand's claim to fame, aside from being old enough to supposedly have been delivered to Marilyn Monroe on the set of her movies, was that it contained only cane sugar and natural ingredients. The whole brand had a very sunny, Southern California vibe to it, and if you grew up in the region during the 1970s or 1980s, you probably had fond memories of it.

The bait we chose to use to start conversations in this case was a Volkswagen 181, more commonly known as the Volkswagen Thing. For those of you who don't know, the Thing was a convertible military vehicle manufactured by VW from 1968 to 1983—and it's funny looking. Picture a Sherman tank crossed with a Jeep Wrangler. It's rare to see one on the street anymore, but it is a favorite of surfers, not only for its quirky looks but because the entire thing can be waterproofed. At the end of a day at the beach, just hose down the interior and let it dry overnight.

So we loaded up one of these Things with cases upon cases of this soda, stuck company logos on either side of the car, and drove it from beach to beach. Sure enough, people would come up and ask us about the car. Eventually they'd say, "What's with the soda stickers?" That was our opening to begin a brand-relevant conversation.

Every day we'd send that car out with a list of 15 to 20 destinations, and every day it would make it to maybe half of them. We had crowds of 50, 60 people lining up to see the car and get a soda. We had to institute a rule: No talking to people who approach you at stoplights." We gave away more soda and started more conversations than we could count.

Yes, you can say we just loaded up a car with soda and handed out freebies. But few start a conversation with you when you're handing out soda from the back of a Nissan Cube or other typical "promo car." As a brand manager, you have to ask yourself, Why is this car right? What is the story here? All the tiny details of what we did pointed directly and specifically toward starting a brand-relevant conversation. A bunch of young people in a Thing who were handing out soda at the beach? What could be more California—thus "brand right" for our client—than that?

Rule 3. Fish Where the Fish Are

You wouldn't fish for sharks in shallow water, and you wouldn't look for NASCAR enthusiasts at a Sephora in Manhattan. You have to throw your bait into the waters frequented by your fish.

Luckily for us, people of similar interests have a tendency to congregate. Figure out where your fish are schooling, and then take your bait to them. Tell your story in a fan forum, drive your new pickup to the parking lot of a monster truck show, or show off your amazing new sweeper in front of parents lining up to see Santa (more on that later).

If you want to catch sharks, you've got to get in a boat and venture into deeper water. And you've got to have huge chunks of big, bloody bait to throw in. Fish where the fish are.

PRO TIP

Internet forums can be good fishing grounds.

Outside of the physical world, Internet forums are the richest, most interesting places to see people having conversations about a shared passion. This is true for a number of reasons. One, forums tend not to skew heavily toward either gender. Two, some forums go all the way back to the LISTSERV days, offering you a comprehensive view of how the conversation has evolved over years, sometimes decades. (For a good example, check out Rennlist, a site for Porsche enthusiasts. That website is essentially a repository for all the Porsche knowledge on earth.)

But the most interesting thing about forums is how they mimic the local PTA meetings, churches, or bars—any small, intimate places where people gather to be part of a community. Want to see this in action? Go to a forum that's been around for a long time and start interacting with the regulars. Just like your first PTA meeting, some will be welcoming. Others will ask you questions, and you will have to exhibit knowledge and genuine interest in the topic before they will accept you. If you know what you are talking about, they will encourage you to start your own thread. Then they will come in, comment on your thread, and ask more questions. And if you try to decline their offer to interact, well, you might as well refuse to bring a dish to the church potluck dinner. Don't be surprised to find yourself on the business end of a cold shoulder.

The truth is, these forums mimic, for better or worse, all the nuances of a face-to-face community. All the glories and grossness of humanity can be seen there. But with all that grossness and glory comes something wonderful: authenticity.

Branded Facebook pages, on the other hand, are not nearly as thick with authentic interactions (also, they tend to skew female). To be sure, brand pages and fan pages serve a purpose, and some are vibrant gathering places for passionate people. But in general, such pages are so clearly dominated by corporate voices that are obviously trying to get site visitors to Like something or to buy something that it's a tough place for people to let their hair down. In general, people go to Facebook brand pages expecting to be sold to, so their defenses are up.

The larger point here is that it's not about digital versus nondigital. It's about authentic versus not authentic. Companies can create forums and Twitter streams that are authentic, but it may be harder than they expect. A company always wants to sell stuff, and it's hard to stop that attitude from coming through. The only thing forum members want to do is share information about something they love. Real influencers can tell the difference.

Catch and Release, and Then Catch Again

Once you've caught your influencers, what are you going to do with them? In many ways, word of mouth marketing is like fishing in a catch-and-release river. You're not going to stuff these influencers and mount them on the wall. You want them to take your bait and go back to where they congregate with like-minded people so they can spread it around. You need to have a system in place so that they can keep coming back for more.

Just as fish will continually return to a spot that contains food, influencers will come back to you if you are constantly supplying interesting, shareable information. Keep feeding them stories, and they will keep coming back.

The most important thing to remember is this: don't chase them. Influencers have a deep desire to identify themselves to you. Your job is to give them as many opportunities as possible to do so and then to feed them what they want. And keep feeding them. That's how you spread your story as effectively as possible to as many people as possible.

As marketers, we need to focus on what the story is and where we're going to throw that story into the water. That is the sum total of what our jobs will be if we're trying to work through people who are influential.

TALKING TO INFLUENCERS

A few years ago, some companies in Asia got busted for putting ground-up gypsum—a mineral commonly used as fertilizer or as a prime ingredient in plaster and drywall—into baby formula. Apparently, it helped make the product more filling. Once caught, they dropped gypsum as an ingredient and then placed stickers on their packaging announcing, "Now gypsum free!"

True? Yes. Authentic? No.

Be Authentic

Influencers are sharers, not sellers. They do not want to be bought, and they will have a negative reaction to anyone they suspect is trying to sell them something. Try it, and you will drive them away.

Influencers can smell PR talk, and they're not interested in it. You have got to approach them with an authentic, believable message, or you will be wasting your time and theirs.

Your story has to be true, and not just cleared-by-the-lawyers true. It has to be honest, and it has to respect your audience's intelligence.

Here's another way to tell when you're being authentic: Most of the time, authenticity is scary to a company. It requires that you share a fairly unvarnished reality, and an unvarnished reality is going to have lumps. In a world where your competition is all basically the same, it may seem like being the same is the safe bet. But once you make the decision not to be that way, you begin to set yourself apart. You create some cognitive dissonance. And that not only gets a customer's attention but it also gets her respect.

To illustrate my point, consider an exception that proves the rule about advertising. In 2009, Domino's Pizza launched a TV campaign that featured real employees listening to real focus groups talk about how awful their pizza was. The word "cardboard" was tossed around like so much shredded mozzarella. These employees, including the CEO, promised to do better. It was how they introduced their new pizza, allegedly redesigned "from the crust up."

That commercial had power because it deviated from the norm—namely, decades of TV commercials featuring cheesy glamour shots of what we all knew were less-than-premium products. Jaded as we are about commercial messages, most of us assumed Domino's knew it was pulling the wool over our eyes (or at least trying) and didn't particularly care as long as the orders kept coming in. Seeing the company's executives get their feelings hurt by criticism of their food was enough to make customers stop and pay attention. That commercial was something to talk about. And who wasn't just a little curious to try that new pizza?

And let's remember: In the Internet age, when everyone is a critic, reporter, and publisher, your company is probably fooling itself if it thinks it can successfully push an inauthentic image of itself. In an age of radical transparency, transparency itself isn't so radical. It's just the smart, honest thing to do.

Still, some people in your company are going to say, "We can't do that. We've never done it that way before." There are going to be people who don't want to do it. So it's going to be hard. You're going to have to have meetings, build a team, be politically astute. But the payoff comes when you start having conversations with consumers, and they see you are being authentic, and they stand up and pay attention. And then they tell their friends about it. The more authentic you are, the more cognitive dissonance you will create. People aren't used to hearing, "Hey, our product could be better, and we're trying to improve it now."

If your story is not authentic, influencers will not share it because that story will hurt their credibility with the people they are trying to influence. This is why you have to deal with influencers in the most authentic way possible. If an influencer smells something that's funny or thinks something is weird, she is not going to share that with her friends.

Trust Them

Advertising is, by its very nature, selective. The creative process for making an ad is focused on emphasizing the appealing elements of your product while leaving out the other stuff.

That is the exact opposite of how you need to approach influencers. You need to give them enough information to do their "job" properly.

Word of mouth marketing can be difficult for advertising people who are trained to stress the positive and ignore the negative or even just to highlight the feature the company wants to talk about. When it comes to influencers, you have to give them as much of the story as you can and let them choose what to talk about. In many ways, that's what you're using them for. They are the ultimate targeting mechanism. They can decide on the spot whom to tell what about your brand, and what not to tell them.

Not because they care about your bottom line. They don't. They care about sharing useful information with their network.

True influencers don't waste people's time by telling, for example, a grandmother about the latest iPhone's cool new social gaming features. A true influencer will tell his grandmother about the phone's new video-chatting app that will let her see and talk to her grandkids on weekends. As a marketer, you have to give her enough information to make that decision.

I have a friend who is a huge fan of all things Disney, particularly the parks. When she goes to a soccer game, she may talk to five different people about what's new at Disney World—and those will be five different conversations. She'll tell the guy who's in danger of losing his job about the new value package, but she'll tell the woman who just made partner about the new bed sheets at the Grand Floridian.

The influencer seeks to always have the most up-to-date and accurate information because she wants to have a continued relationship with the people she's influencing. She wants to be a resource. And she wants to be a resource because she's superinterested and superpassionate about her thing, whether it be Disney World or wine or tropical fish.

The more aspects of your story and the more pieces of the puzzle you give to an influencer, the more able she is to put those pieces together in a way that is relevant to the person she is talking to. In that way, influencers are more efficient than a company ever could be. They will nearly always send a very targeted message directly to the appropriate person.

No one has ever written an algorithm that is more efficient, accurate, or reliable than the human brain.

Also bear in mind that these people are storytellers. What respectable storyteller would tell the story of Goldilocks without the scary part where the bears get angry about the intruder? Nobody wants to hear, or tell, half a story. So you have to tell a complete one, not just the parts you want to emphasize.

Start Being Patient Now

The path that information travels when spread by an influencer can be a very circuitous one. Unlike your television commercial, it is not being pushed in someone's face during every timeout of every Sunday NFL game. The information spreads at its own organic, socially acceptable pace. This requires something else marketers—and frankly, their bosses—aren't known for: patience.

Let's say you and I are friends. In reality, we will probably get together, what, every two months? Maybe less? Now let's say I know that you love barbecue sauce every bit as much as I do. Does that mean I am going to call you the moment I find out about a new flavor or recipe? Probably not. In the grand scheme of things, it's just not that important. More likely, I will wait until I see you again, and then I will make a point of telling you about it. And you might not act on the new information until I ask you if you've tried it when I see you again two months later.

When left to its own devices, word of mouth travels at a leisurely pace. Sometimes, as in the case of a new movie, that pace is a fast one because time is a factor. Otherwise, it can wait. So we have to as well. With rare exceptions, you can't share stories with an influencer today and expect to see your sales increase a month from today. Word of mouth requires patience.

Don't think that information traveling at a slower, more natural pace will somehow make less of an impact once it finds its target. On the contrary, that organic pace gives word of mouth marketing its power because it's so unlike in-your-face advertising. Word of mouth marketing is shared willingly and naturally. The listener's defenses aren't up; he is receptive to new information. In-your-face advertising makes people feel bombarded. Word of mouth makes them feel like they are part of the club.

This is one reason it's important to plan your word of mouth campaigns far in advance, to work with influencers as early as you can. You can't force a seed to grow into a plant more quickly. Plant the seed today and reap the harvest later. Give a Disney fanatic information about the park and trust that, when the time comes, the information will find its mark. Because even if it's been months since I've seen my friend who knows everything about Disney, whom do you think I'm going to call if I do plan a trip to Orlando? That's when your seed will bear fruit.

But first, you have to plant the seed. How do you do that with influencers? It requires a little bit of generosity on your part. It requires you to give them a taste. As we'll discuss in the next chapter, it requires you to give them their two-ounce sample.

CHAPTER 2

The Two-Ounce Culture: Why Smart Brands Sample

CASE STUDY: SUGARLAND

All bands give away concert tickets to fans. In 2009, Sugarland took the process to a whole new level, giving away pairs of tickets to anyone who cared to look for them—and sharing a little of themselves in the process.

First, some background.

Sugarland is a country music duo with a twist. As any fan of the genre can tell you, country music these days is divided between purists and mainstream fans. The latter group is more likely to embrace a Taylor Swift or a Brad Paisley, while the former casts a suspicious eye on any artist who can't speak at length on the virtues of Waylon Jennings or Patsy Cline. If you're going to play country music these days, you can expect to be judged—harshly—on which side of the border you fall. Most country acts work hard to establish their country bona fides.

Sugarland, a client of ours, openly flouts this divide. They don't try to disguise their love for rock music or the influence it's had on them and their sound. This is the essence of who Sugarland

is—fans of eclectic music who grew up to become musicians—
and they embrace it.

This includes their approach to giving away concert tickets.
Traditionally, before a country music artist plays a show, he or she
will go on the local country radio station and give away a pair of
tickets to the ninety-fifth caller, or whatever number corresponds
to the station's call letters. But true to Sugarland's eclectic philosophy, they wanted to be more inclusive than that. Why just offer
tickets to country music fans (or fast dialers) when you could offer
them to—anyone at all?

On their 2009 "Love on the Inside" tour, the members of Sugarland, Kristian Bush and Jennifer Nettles, videotaped themselves
hiding a pair of tickets in the Walmart closest to the arena. Then
they uploaded the video online with a vague description of where
to find the tickets. ("I think they're in aisle 15," for example.) It was
more fun than a radio station giveaway, but also more inclusive.
Anyone could go and find those tickets and check out a Sugarland
show for free.

Though they would never consider themselves marketers,
Kristian and Jennifer are two people who understand the value of
samples. The best way to lure people into your "tribe" is by first
giving them a sample of what you have to offer. Here are some free
tickets to come check out our band. Maybe you'll like us, maybe
you won't. Sample our music and decide for yourself.

But there was more to these giveaways than letting people
into concerts. The videos themselves were samples of the Sugarland "brand." As I noted, Sugarland is all about flouting the rules,
about being your authentic self regardless of what others expect.
In one video, Jennifer is wearing a Beatles T-shirt, and Kristian is
wearing a Bruce Springsteen T-shirt—not bands that are typically

revered in all country music circles. And Jennifer appears busy and possibly even disheveled. She pokes fun at her own tousled appearance.

"I'm in disguise," she says, laughing, from the back of a car, "because I have on my T-shirt and my zits. These aren't really my zits. These are just for disguise, to look like ordinary folks. Along with the dirty hair. My hair is resplendent underneath this slicked-back ponytail and zits." Find and watch the video. It's an object lesson in creating talkable stories from the every day.

Even more so than the tickets, such videos were a great way to let people sample Sugarland. Anyone who came across them would see a cool, authentic, fun pair of musicians who treat fans the way they themselves would want to be treated by their musical heroes. Kristian and Jennifer figured out what was unique about them, and they found a fun, talkable way to share it.

In a world dominated by conversation, this is the way to lure people into your brand's orbit. Figure out what makes it special, and then let people have a taste of that in a fun, shareable way. It may sound unorthodox, but in fact, it's what consumers have come to expect.

- - - - - - - - - - -

Average brands advertise. Great brands share.

When was the last time you drank three of the same beers in a row?

It's a simple question, but a revealing one. Ask yourself. Ask your friends. Hell, ask your bartender. When is the last time you had three of the same beers in a row?

Let me guess: it's been a while.

It's a question I often ponder when I find myself at beer festivals, an occupational hazard that comes from having clients in the beverage industry. As you probably know, beer festivals are not great places to grab a pint of your favorite brew and hang out with friends. They are venues for finding new flavors and varieties, expanding your knowledge and your palate, tasting as many different beers as you can till you find one that speaks to you. Then starting all over again.

In short, beer festival culture is all about sampling. And the standard size for those samples is about two ounces. Ask to taste a particular beer, and you'll be presented with a two-ounce pour on which to base your decision. Do you want a full glass? Or is this brew not for you? Maybe try two ounces of something else first? Then try two more?

Over the past 20 years, beer festival culture has slowly infected the overall beer culture in America. Sure, we all still have our favorite brands or varieties. My first beer of the night will almost always be a stout of some kind. My wife will always start with a wheat beer. Certain thirtysomethings in Portland will always start with a PBR, and maybe even follow up with another. But three in a row? There are just too many options available.

This is a far cry from the beer culture of 1950s America, when there were maybe four brands of beer for sale, and they were all pretty similar to one another.

What happened?

THE RISE OF THE SAMPLE CULTURE

Before World War II, beer in America was all about consistency—a major challenge before the advent of refrigerated trucking. As a highly perishable product, beer could travel only so far before it turned into carbonated garbage. So brands like Miller and Busch made their fortunes by establishing nationwide networks of breweries that could produce a clean, hearty product that tasted the same in Dallas, Texas, as it did in Portland, Maine. In an age of varying quality and limited product choices, consistency was the key to winning customer loyalty.

Of course, imports existed, as did smaller, specialty brews. But they were expensive and hard to find, and you could never really be sure of their quality—particularly if they had traveled from far away. Such niche items were for the true connoisseurs, or maybe a special occasion. But go to a friend's house and ask for a Belgian wheat, and you stood a pretty good chance of losing a friend.

No, Budweiser was your beer. Or Miller. Or later, maybe Miller Lite. If you were drinking beer, you drank your brand, can after can after can.

In the late 1980s, things began to change. Small craft breweries were producing more exotic and flavorful beers, which captured the attention of younger and more adventurous beer drinkers. And because it was different—it came from different parts of the country—each beer had its own taste, texture, and color. Breweries employed long-neglected brewing methods to create a more interesting and authentic product, and customers loved telling their friends about it. Craft beer wasn't just a new product category. It was a collection of great stories that fans were excited to share.

As these beers made their way across the country and they became available in more and more stores, the cost of trying something new—both in terms of money and effort expended—began to drop. You didn't have to seek it out. It was no longer prohibitively expensive. Trying an alternative brew became easier.

A few years later came Internet access, which turbocharged the spread of the craft beer story. On dedicated beer forums and message boards, but also in unrelated venues like music or travel chat rooms, people eagerly told tales of their favorite local brews. Friends told friends, strangers told strangers, and word spread. And a whole lot of beer was sold.

Soon, to a new generation of beer drinkers, the idea of drinking nothing but, say, Coors Light—followed by another Coors Light, and then another—was unthinkable. The point was always to be tasting something new. The craft beer revolution had taken hold.

In 1980, craft brewers in the United States produced 26,000 barrels of beer, according to the Brewers Association. By 2012, that number had risen to 13,235,917 barrels, accounting for 6.5 percent of total U.S. beer sales by volume and 10.2 percent by dollars.[1] In early 2014, craft beer accounted for about 30 percent of Costco's beer sales.

And if you ever need proof, talk to a young beer drinker. Ask him when was the last time he drank three of the same beer in a row.

Then ask yourself, would my marketing strategy have any effect on the choices this person makes?

Consumers Want Their Two-Ounce Samples

I tell the beer story to illustrate how Americans have changed their approach to buying over the past 50 years. Today, beer drinkers are hardly the only ones demanding their two-ounce samples. Foodies, bookworms, music fans, movie buffs, even porn enthusiasts are loathe to spend a dime before they have had a taste.

It is a fundamental change in how purchasing decisions are made by American consumers, and it affects nearly every aspect of our lives. The number of options has expanded so widely while the cost of sampling has plummeted so much that we now have the luxury of browsing to our heart's content. Try a little of this, try a little of that. Commitment can wait.

In turn, the old ways of advertising no longer make sense. Simply telling people about your product won't cut it. In a two-ounce culture, you need to get your product into people's hands. You have to recognize that they want to explore their options, which means you have to give them a taste first.

Take a look at how our approach to dating has changed in recent years.

Once upon a time, your dating pool was limited to the people you had actually met or heard about from your friends or family. Assuming you were willing to date only people who were roughly your age and not already married, that was a relatively limited number of options—particularly if you lived in a small town or had a small social circle.

Matchmakers and personal ads expanded your options some- what, but at a snail's pace. Personal ads were tiny and rarely in- cluded photos; matchmakers knew only so many people, and they could send you on only so many dates at once.

If you found someone worth dating, you spent time with that person—face-to-face, or at least on the phone—in order to learn more. Is she close to her family? Does he want to have children? Does she share your taste in music? If you wanted to experience that person, you had to go on an actual date.

The Internet, specifically sites like Match.com, changed ev- erything. Now, we can scan endless pages of multimedia personal ads—pictures, testimonials, likes, dislikes, hobbies, income— before we commit to even a single date. We reject hundreds if not thousands of potential mates based on nothing but digital previews. Before we will commit to a single cocktail, we browse through seemingly endless options, weighing the pros and cons and seeing what suits us.

When we finally arrive at that date, we show up more informed about our companion than any person from the 1980s who didn't work for the FBI ever could have imagined. We have made the smallest of commitments—a single night out—only after many hours of searching and considering and rejecting.

In short, we have sampled our options. Exhaustively. Because we can.

It's true of nearly any industry or human activity you can name these days. Want to read a new book? Start with a free sample from iTunes or the Kindle library. Curious about a new restaurant? Buy the Groupon and try it for half-off. Looking for a new home? Take virtual tours of dozens of listings in your city, whether or not you can afford them. And I won't even get into the many ways of nefariously "sampling" every piece of music ever recorded before deciding if you want to purchase a song, much less a whole album. (When's the last time you did *that*?) The same is true for nearly every movie and TV show ever made.

Why Has Sampling Triumphed?

Because of technology and the proliferation of brands, it's a sampling culture that we live in. And we are never, ever going back. We, as marketers, need to deal with that.

Technology
How did we get here? One obvious answer is technology. Widespread broadband access, smartphones, digital cameras and

recording equipment, MP3s, Internet-based publishing plat-forms, on-demand television—the list goes on and on. Thanks to the digital revolution, it is cheaper and easier than ever to produce and consume—or merely browse through—nearly everything.

Think about the state of photography. Anyone over 30 will re-member a time when taking a picture was a pretty big deal. You had to line up your shot, make sure the lighting was correct, and make everyone say "cheese" at precisely the same moment. Why? Because film was expensive! You had 24 or 36 pictures per roll, so you had to make each one count. Worse, you had no idea whether your pictures were any good until you got them developed, a pro-cess that cost nearly as much as the film.

Only the most wealthy or reckless among us would run around snapping pictures indiscriminately. You'd go broke in a week.

Today's iPhone has a feature that allows the user to hold a but-ton for a few short seconds and capture dozens of pictures at once. Hold it a bit longer and you'll end up with hundreds. The camera then automatically chooses the best one for you. If you disagree with that choice, you can manually scroll through all those pic-tures, choosing the ones you like and deleting the ones you don't. Or keep them all. Who cares? The iPhone can store thousands of photos. Or download them onto your laptop, which can hold hundreds of thousands.

The point is, the cost of taking a picture is literally a microfrac-tion of what it used to be. As a result, we take many, many more of them. Why not? There is little to no risk or cost involved.

It's an example of how technology has made it easier to con-sume and produce once-costly things. But it's also a metaphor.

The way we take pictures today is like the way we try new things: haphazardly, with little to no sense of risk or cost.

Because it is so much less expensive to try something new, people are trying a lot more things. If you're curious about skydiving, you can start out with some first-person skydiving videos online. Maybe you can't make it to Pamplona this year, but you can spend an afternoon watching videos of tourists wearing Go Pros running with the bulls. Last year, as we were planning a trip to Brazil, my wife spent her evenings online sampling everything there is to do in the three towns we were going to visit. Twenty years ago, finding all that information would have taken six months of deep library work, and even then she would have come up short. Now she can look at films, slide shows, user reviews—she did everything but taste and smell our vacation before we even made a hotel reservation.

The Proliferation of Brands

The other reason sampling is so easy now is that there are simply so many more choices. That is why sharing has now become so much more important. Gone are the days when there were two beers to choose from, or three TV shows, or four kinds of candy bars. The cost of producing and marketing new products has sunk so low that the shelves are full to bursting with new options. Faced with a dozen new kinds of chewing gum, who among us won't give something new a try now and then?

These days, very little is holding us back from trying something previously unavailable to us. This is both very good, and very bad, for your brand. Which is why it's more important than ever for you to have a great story to share.

It's Time to Adapt

Adapting to this sampling culture can mean the life or death of your brand. Sound extreme? Compare the case of beer brewers to that of the record companies.

Brewers

When it comes to embracing sampling culture, few industries can hold a candle to beer brewers. Again, this is best encapsulated by their approach to beer festivals. Throw a festival, and brewers will happily show up with their various brews and recipes, which they are happy to share with whoever shows an interest. And it's not just the beer. Brewers all seem to have beards and clothes that somehow reflect the ethos of their beers. The implication is that choosing their brand means joining their tribe. Maybe you want to belong, maybe not. Either way, here is a chance to give it a try.

If you don't care for a particular beer, the brewer will more than likely tell you about a colleague—a competitor, in fact—who brews something you might prefer. He might even tell you he's been kicking himself for not coming up with the competitor's beer first. But he's not going to copy that beer because that's not what his brewery is about. But hey, why don't you go give it a try? You might like it as much as he does.

Thanks to that kind of attitude, the Great American Beer Festival in Denver, for example, has grown from a small industry gathering to a nationally recognized event that attracts tens of thousands of beer drinkers—and seemingly as many brewers. The beer industry is teeming with brands, fans, and success stories. People today love to talk about their beers and love to hear about beers they haven't tried yet. And you can expect to get your two-ounce sample not only at beer festivals but at pretty much any bar that is serious about beer. This is what can happen when you embrace the sampling culture.

Recording Companies

Then there is the recording industry, which has done more to fight the culture of sampling than any industry I can think of. And it has not worked out well for them.

For record companies, the world began to change in the early 2000s, when it suddenly became easy to sample music. Napster, Gnutella, Kazaa. All these peer-to-peer file-sharing services gave consumers the freedom to share their music collections with anyone around the world. The record companies' reaction? They whined about how easy it had become to sample music, and they did everything in their power to stop it.

Of course, they had a legitimate gripe. The product they had paid millions of dollars to produce was being downloaded for free—not a problem the brewers ever had. But rather than seeing this seismic shift as an opportunity to change the way they deal with customers, record companies refused to look beyond the piracy aspect. When they saw kids downloading music, they didn't see lifelong superfans on the cutting edge of music distribution. They saw thieves, and they treated them as such. Instead of adapting to the new reality, they sponsored legislation that made downloading music a crime, paid people to populate file-sharing services with bad copies of their own products, attempted to shut down the sites themselves, and most infamously, had teenagers arrested for downloading music.

As you probably already know, this approach did not work. And suing teenagers who love music was not great for the industry's reputation either, particularly among teenagers who love music.

Steve Jobs saw things differently. When he saw teenagers sharing songs on the Internet, he didn't see thieves. He saw enthusiastic music fans who were fulfilling the dream of owning all the music in the world at little to no cost. He saw kids who were downloading music they had never heard before, or would never have considered listening to, simply because the cost was so low and the effort so minimal. He saw potential customers.

He also saw that the file-sharing services were not perfect: Viruses abounded. It could be difficult to find the music you wanted. And they were far too technically complex for those of us no longer in our twenties.

What if, he imagined, he could create a place where people could download music easily and safely and have to pay only $0.99 per song? Who wouldn't part with $0.99, particularly if it meant music files that were guaranteed to be safe?

iTunes worked because the people downloading music weren't interested in being criminals. They were interested in music. And it turns out that most people will happily pay a small price to get the music they're looking for without having to work too hard or worry about hurting their computers—or steal. Jobs embraced the sampling behavior that the recording industry fought.

I'm not saying the record companies would be raking in huge profits these days had they done the same. Technology changed, and much about their old business model was rendered obsolete. However, they did themselves no favors by fighting a futile war against an unstoppable cultural shift.

There is good sampling, and there is bad sampling.

When working with the Atlanta Hawks, we saw that starting conversations about a sports team can be tough if it's not currently in the finals or threatening to leave the city. If you're not a sports fan, what's talkable about a basketball team? It turns out that the team's interaction with the community can make for good conversation, but the actions have got to be compelling. "Good sampling" is any activation that will compel influencers to share your brand story with their friends.

One potentially talkable asset we had noticed at the games was the mascot, Harry the Hawk. Fans, especially kids, loved Harry. The adults —you know, the actual ticket buyers— thought Harry was fun, but the in-game antics of a pro sports mascot aren't really talkable the day after the game.

One day, during a brand onboarding process we go through with our clients, we found a picture of Harry the Hawk that sparked an epiphany. Once, the guy who plays Harry had been running late for a game, so he rode to work on his motorcycle in full mascot regalia. That's something you don't see every day, so naturally people whipped out their cameras and started taking photos of him. They probably even told their friends about it later.

So we thought, What if we put Harry out in the community doing everyday things? What if we had him running errands, just as we all do, but errands very specific to him? He could go to Whole Foods and buy birdseed. He could wait in line at the mall for the new iPhone. What if we just had Harry going out and doing stuff that Atlantans do every day? What if we created a whole program around "Everyday Harry"?

That's what we did. Harry would show up at Whole Foods unannounced and do his shopping. He would buy a huge amount of birdseed, so it was a good visual, and he would shake his head when he walked past the poultry aisle. We sent Harry to a beauty salon to get an actual haircut (we used an old mascot suit). Harry watched NFL games in a sports bar and waited in line at midnight when the latest Xbox game was released. Etc., etc., etc., ad infinitum.

Naturally, people swarmed Harry—and not just kids. Full-grown adults wanted Harry's autograph. People took pictures and shared them on Twitter and Facebook. It's not every day you see a 7-foot-tall Hawk shopping in your local store or riding his motorcycle. Before long, we were getting calls from parade and festival organizers asking for Harry appearances. Salon owners who saw Harry's haircut wanted him to come to their stores. The whole community was embracing Harry, regardless of the Hawks' win-loss record. And before long, metrics for the Hawks started to change.

The Atlanta Hawks want to fill seats and expose potential fans to the team. For many teams, the default marketing tactics revolve around ticket giveaways, in-game freebies, and discounts on marginal products like tickets in the rafters (these would be examples of "bad sampling" because they don't focus on creating conversation; they focus on value

(continues)

shifting). Rather than going this route, the Atlanta Hawks chose to spend money on sharing their brand story with the community and doing things that would start conversations about the team. Now they are reaping the rewards. We only had to identify what would get people talking about their brand and put it out in the community.

The Choice: The Record Companies or the Brewers

It comes down to this: Now that we live in this two-ounce culture, are you going to be the record companies, or will you be the brewers? Will you come to grips with this situation and work with it, or are you going to work against it? Because when you work against it, you lose. How much smaller is the record music industry today? In 2012, total U.S. album sales were 316 million units. That's down from 617 million in 1996. The bestselling album of 2013 sold fewer than 2.5 million copies. That wouldn't have cracked the top 10 in 1985.

Fighting the urge to sample won't get you very far. The trick is learning how to make money from it.

THE VERY GOOD (AND VERY BAD) NEWS FOR YOUR BRAND

Question: In a world where consumers are faced with a thousand different choices, any of which they can sample at almost any time, at little to no cost or risk, what is keeping them loyal to your brand?

Answer: Very, very little.

The Consequences of Consumers Having Choices

It is a simple truth of modern consumerism: nearly every product category is full to bursting with competing brands, each laser focused on appealing to a certain kind of consumer. Not happy with your mainstream cable company? Try that sports-centric satellite service, or cut the cable altogether and buy your programming piecemeal from Amazon.com and iTunes. Worried about the environmental impact of your plastic diapers? Try the ecofriendly brand—there is one available in nearly every store—or sign up online for your local cloth diaper delivery service. It takes just a few seconds, and there is a guaranteed trial period during which you can change your mind for free.

As a culture, we have evolved into this two-ounce mindset, and that has put a serious drain on brand loyalty. That means different things to your brand depending on what you're selling and what you're trying to accomplish. But either way, you have got to adjust.

This erosion of brand loyalty has three major effects on brands.

Older, Established Brands Need to Work Harder

For legacy brands, the facts that the cost of switching brands has lowered, options have exploded, and consumers are obsessed with sampling clearly spell bad news. Mostly.

Consider the case of Ragú spaghetti sauces. When I was growing up, there was no more authentic spaghetti sauce in the grocery store than Ragú. As a kid, that heavy red jar was the height of Italian cuisine. Many other Americans felt similarly. But the fact was, we didn't know any better. Ragú was, for all intents and purposes, the finest thing on the shelf. If my family wanted a quality Italian meal but didn't want to spend two days making a meat sauce, Ragú was it.

Today, there are 31 different brands of spaghetti sauce on the shelf at my local grocery store. Some have no preservatives. Some are organic. Some are designed to look as if they were jarred yesterday by a grandmother in Sheepshead Bay, Brooklyn. Some are meant to appeal to kids.

Faced with those options, even the most loyal consumer would be tempted to stray. Maybe you try a new sauce, find something you like better, and switch forever. Maybe you find something that you serve just to your kids. Maybe you add a couple of new sauces to your family's rotation. Maybe you stray only once, and then return forever to Ragú.

The point is, in any of these scenarios, Ragú loses, even if it's just a little bit. A previously loyal customer gave his money to a competitor, even just once, because he was presented with options. Most legacy brands have built their businesses to focus obsessively on not letting that happen. Today the two-ounce mindset requires these brands to think differently.

Your customers are going to wander. You're going to spring leaks. The question is how you plug them.

Startups or Niche Players Have an Advantage, but Only at First

Now, imagine you are one of those newer spaghetti sauces. Congratulations, this is your age of glory. It has never been easier to get someone to try something new. Today, consumers want to try your product simply because it *is* new. How great is that?

In a two-ounce culture, where people are constantly presented with new options, consumers are more likely to seek out the advice of their influencer friends. They want to hear stories about these new brands they've heard of. Like everyone else, they are in search of new experiences and tastes, but they don't have time to waste on unworthy products. So they talk to more people in search of experiences and recommendations. If they're going to take a vacation, they're going to speak with their well-traveled relative first. If they're unsure what book to read next, they're going to ask their buddy the bookworm. If they're looking for a restaurant in which to celebrate their anniversary, they're going to consult with their foodie friend.

This is great news for startups and other young companies. Rather than looking askance at the new product on the shelves, consumers these days are more likely to be intrigued and want to give it a try.

The problem is getting them to stick. In an age of constant sampling, you have to give your customers a reason not to take their two ounces and move on to the next thing. You need to give them a quality product—but you also need to give them a great story. Your story, backed up by word of mouth, is what turns a sampler into a loyal customer.

And just like legacy brands, newer brands also have to stay on their toes. They, too, must always be innovating. In a two-ounce culture, the speed at which you move from hot new thing to old fuddy-duddy has increased exponentially. How long did it take Starbucks to morph from hip underground brand out of Seattle to the McDonald's of coffee? To the extent that Starbucks has held on, it is because it has continued to innovate. And the same is true of any brand, old or new, trying to survive in a sample-mad culture.

Brand Extensions and Innovation Are More Important Than Ever

Here's where the established brands have an edge over startups: in addition to a name that consumers know and trust, older brands have the resources to invest in research and development. And never before has the return on investment for innovation been greater.

I'm not talking about innovation for innovation's sake. I'm talking about the kind that makes CFOs sleep better at night, the kind that brings in more money this quarter than last quarter.

Because sampling is so inexpensive now, it is going to be more and more common for people to want to sample a variety of things. And if you as an existing company know that, you can feed it with brand extensions, new products, and true innovations. Get them in front of the consumer, and the consumer will try it. And that means that the dollars you invest in innovation are going to be more valuable for you than ever before.

Take Boston Brewing, the company that makes Sam Adams beer. The Boston Lager is its flagship item. In addition to that, it has dozens of other brews, some seasonal, some in production year-round, that consumers are always looking to sample. Maybe those other brews make up 15 percent of the company's overall sales. But if that 15 percent is what's always new and always interesting and it is attracting more people to the brand, then it's a good investment.

If sampling were expensive and difficult, you wouldn't have to do all these things. But sampling is inexpensive, and consumers' brand switching costs are low. So people are naturally going to try things, and a certain percentage of them are going to find something they like, and a certain percentage of them are going to be influential. So if you are an existing brand, you must continue to innovate and give customers something new to share.

You must move from sampling to sharing if you're going to build relationships. Your customers are going to wander. It's a fact of modern consumerism. It's your job to keep them from wandering to another brand entirely, to give them enough new and exciting products to try, and to get samples of those products into their hands.

The shift to a two-ounce culture mindset is an opportunity to refocus your company on the idea of innovation. Done right, every dollar you spend on innovation today is going to yield greater benefit than it would have 40, or even 20, years ago.

The Innovation Vortex

That said, you must beware of the *innovation vortex*—that is, being in a state of constantly dreaming up new extensions and "innovations" that eventually fail to make an impact. Mattel is a marvelous company that has done spectacular things with its multi-billion-dollar Barbie brand.

But the sheer volume of different Barbies for sale, not to mention her cars and homes and boyfriends, plus the special anniversary dolls, have long since made the dolls a comedy cliché. At this point, the new extensions cease to really be innovations. I'm sure there are economic advantages to producing these products. But if you're producing new brand extensions simply to have something new on the shelf, they are not going to generate much conversation.

Luckily, the right story can keep you from falling into the innovation vortex.

WHERE YOUR BRAND'S STORY FITS IN

For companies looking to sell something, the two-ounce culture can be a double-edged sword. On the one hand, it is an opportunity to attract new customers. Because people are looking to try something different, it gives companies a chance to constantly be introducing their products and stories to new people. Engaging potential customers is easier than ever. That's the wonderful part of being in business today and the reason it's important to be comfortable with the sampling culture.

On the other hand, a sampling culture encourages people to constantly move on, to always be in search of that next best thing. It's hard to build much of a customer base in that kind of environment. Getting people to sample is easy; getting them to stay is hard.

Sharing Makes Your Story Sticky

This is where your brand's story comes in. It is your story, told and reinforced by an influencer or group of influencers, that gets people to stick. "I've already told you this is the best product in the category," says the influencer. "This is what *we* use. Why are you still trying those other things?"

A few years back, I was having a drink in a cop bar when I saw something that perfectly encapsulates this point. Everyone in this bar was drinking Pabst Blue Ribbon. Apparently, it was the preferred beer of the regulars—and everyone in this bar was a regular. Then, in walks a trainee and his training officer. The training officer, of course, orders a Pabst Blue Ribbon. The trainee, however, ordered a Miller Lite.

It was one of those drag-the-needle-across-the-record mo-ments. Everything stopped. All the other officers with their PBRs paused their conversations to look at the new kid who was order-ing the funny beer. Eventually, the kid noticed the disapproving looks and changed his drink order.

The cops in that bar had long since decided, as a tribe, what they were about. And the message to the trainee was, "If you're going to be part of this tribe, you're going to drink what we drink."

We may not all have a bar full of cops to enforce the purchase of our products, but we do have access to influencers and their networks. By constantly providing these influencers with stories about your brand and what makes it cool, you can turn them into your very own bar full of cops. Make enough influencers in a sin-gle tribe love your brand, and anyone who wants to be a member of that tribe will be embarrassed to order anything else. Those sto-ries can be any number of things: innovations, some cool (and au-thentic!) promotion with a band, or treating your employees well. These are the sorts of things that generate word of mouth, that keep influencers talking about how great your brand is. It can be the reason people decide to sample your brand, and it can also be the reason they stay. Word of mouth makes your story sticky.

As important as it is to embrace the sampling culture, it is just as important ultimately to get off the sampling carousel. For ob-vious reasons, you don't want your customers perpetually living off your free two-ounce samples. It is the compelling story, shared enthusiastically among friends, that engenders loyalty, that says, "This is our brand. We are done sampling those other things. By showing your loyalty to this, you prove yourself to be part of our tribe." You only have to find your story and get it into the proper hands.

Making a Good Story a Great One

A good story will attract people. A great story will keep them.

A truly great story is one that can constantly be refreshed. Can you keep your story interesting? Can you keep adding interesting details that enrich and deepen your story? Can you keep adding new ways to think about it without being repetitive? That's a great story.

In advertising, they talk about The Big Idea. It's that tag line or concept—Nike's Just Do It, Volkswagen's Think Small, the Marlboro Man—that can keep on delivering, that hits on something so elemental it resonates widely across language and time. Great stories are a lot like that. They can be told over and over again from different perspectives and with varying details, yet always remain compelling and resonant.

This is the world we now live in. Just as technology does not go backward, our taste for sampling will never be quenched or abandoned. You cannot put the toothpaste back in the tube. If you want to reach the maximum number of people, if you want to be the brewers, not the music industry, you need to get your product into as many hands as possible. You need to provide your two-ounce samples. And those samples must come with a story that can be shared long after the sample is gone. And that story should be one you can tell again and again, a hundred different ways. That is how you get people to join your tribe, and how you will keep them from wandering. It starts with samples, but it ends with great stories.

CHAPTER 3

What Makes You Talkable? Finding Your Brand's Story

CASE STUDY: ACADEME OF THE OAKS

In Chapter 1, I told you about the Academe of the Oaks, the Atlanta private school that was having trouble generating word of mouth. Part of the problem was that the school was offering a $500 reward to anyone who referred a friend, which turned out to be a disincentive to true influencers, who are loathe to be seen as salespeople. But having the school discontinue that practice was just one change we helped the school make.

When Academe came to us, the school was struggling to differentiate itself from other private schools in the area. The message it was putting out in print ads and on brochures was about small classes and personal attention. But these are the same things all private schools advertise. In fact, if you're sending your kid to a private school, you probably assume it will provide small classes and personal attention. Our job was to identify what made Academe different—what made it talkable—and put that out into the community.

We didn't have to spend much time with the folks at Academe before we found that point of differentiation. It was the school's faculty. The philosophy of the woman who founded Academe was that all teachers should be experts in the subjects that they taught. That may sound obvious, but you'd be surprised by how many, say, English teachers in the United States don't have a degree in English. Many teachers, even at private schools, have education degrees. All the teachers at Academe had proven expertise in their field; many of them even had PhDs. That was not only unusual among private schools but it was also a great conversation starter.

After we convinced Academe to do away with the $500 referral reward, we came up with ways to get the community talking about its teachers.

Academe adopted our suggestion that the faculty participate in trivia nights at the local burgers-and-beers joint. Each week, four teachers from four different disciplines formed a team called Academe, and the team competed against the locals. Naturally, they won—a lot. Others in the restaurant wanted to know who these people were and why they were so good. That launched a hundred conversations about the school and the superior qualifications of its faculty.

The Decatur Book Festival is the largest independent book festival in the country. Every August, more than a thousand published authors come to Decatur to read and promote their work. Starting in 2011, we encouraged Academe to forgo its usual booth at the festival and instead have students hold sidewalk readings of their own material. Clad in Academe T-shirts, students showed up with microphones on street corners around the festival and read or performed their own essays, poems, plays, or short stories.

Huge crowds gathered, and at the end of each performance, the student said, "Brought to you by Academe!" to huge applause. They've now done this several years in a row, and it always starts tons of conversations among parents and potential students.

Following on the festival theme, we suggested faculty members compile thought-provoking quotes, mathematical equations, and scientific facts and write them in chalk on high-traffic sidewalks. They'd write things like, "What was Alfred Nobel [as in the Nobel Prize] famous for inventing?" Then a few blocks later, they would write the answer—"Dynamite!"—and they'd sign it with "Academe of the Oaks." These were not only topics of conversation among festivalgoers but also games: some people would walk around trying to find every one.

We encouraged faculty members to participate in Dragon Con's annual Saturday morning parade. If you're not familiar with Dragon Con, it is a giant science fiction and fantasy convention that takes place in Atlanta every year. One of the most popular parts of the convention is the Saturday morning parade, in which attendees march through downtown Atlanta dressed in some of the craziest and most impressive costumes you've ever seen. Each year, a group of locals dress as the Periodic Table of the Elements. The guy representing copper might wear a police uniform (Get it? Copper?), while the lady dressed as francium would wear a beret and carry a baguette. We encouraged the teachers to join that group. Because the costumes aren't always obvious, these folks tend to have a lot of conversations about them while they're walking, and those conversations eventually wind around to a marcher's professional life (because who exactly does something like this?). Lots of the people in and around that parade have a child or a friend with a child who is considering private school.

Finally, we helped train the parents. Taking to heart the lesson of the failed $500 referral reward, we brought in parents who would want to recommend the school to their friends and talked to them about how to share their stories. Again, no influencer wants to be seen as a salesperson, so we helped make parents comfortable going out and talking about their experiences with the school without feeling like they were being pushy.

After implementing these tactics, Academe found its enrollment outlook changing. It met its five-year goal by the end of the second year of our program. Getting in is a lot harder than it used to be, and many good students end up on a waiting list. The school is looking for ways to expand, possibly with more land or a new building. And all because it told a different story about itself.

That story was always there. But the school's leadership couldn't see it because they weren't thinking in terms of story. They knew that it cost them a lot of money and headaches to keep class sizes small and that "personal attention" looked good in magazine ads. But it turns out that people do not choose their child's private school based on magazine ads. They choose it based on what other parents are saying. Our program worked because it gave parents in the community something great to say about Academe. Picture yourself at a Sunday brunch. With you are people you know—a friend of a friend, a woman you used to work with, maybe your accountant—but not people you're particularly close to. These people are all busy and naturally preoccupied with their own lives.

You're going to tell them a story. Will it keep them interested? Will they lean in as you talk? Will they nod their heads and widen their eyes, flashing a little smile as you reach your conclusion?

Or will they start to look around the room before you've barely said a word? Will their attention wander? Will they interrupt in hopes of changing the topic? Will they ask questions not to learn more but to poke holes in your premise? Will they start a side conversation before you've had a chance to make your point?

The fact is that anyone can tell a story. The trick in word of mouth marketing is coming up with one that others want to share with people. Even if they did not show up that day to hear what it is you're talking about.

This is particularly hard when the story is about your business. It's kind of like talking about your own child. What you find fascinating can be glaze-over boring to others. You have to choose and craft such stories carefully, with your audience in mind.

FINDING YOUR BRAND'S STORY

If you're going to share your story with influencers, you need to make it *talkable*. That's a word we use at Fizz to mean, simply, something that people will want to talk about. Just because you're talking doesn't mean what you're saying is talkable.

The Talkable Story

For a story to be talkable, it has to be three things: relevant, interesting, and authentic. Fail on any one of these points, and your story probably won't be shared. Let's look at each point individually.

Relevant

Think back to what we know about influencers. Why do they share stories? Because they want to create or deepen their relationships with the people they are talking to. Influencers do what they do as an expression of love. This is why they maintain the largest possible networks of friends and influencees.

A true influencer won't try sharing a story he doesn't think is relevant to the person he is talking to. Think about it: Would you tell your mother-in-law about the enhanced game play in *Call of Duty 4*? Would that story help build a stronger relationship between the two of you? Her takeaway from such a conversation might be that you don't know her very well and that you haven't taken the time to consider what interests her. That is not how influencers—who, let's remember, have strong social skills—work. If they're going to tell someone a story, they are going to be sure it is about something that person is interested in, so it will strengthen the bond between them.

If it's going to be talkable, the story of your brand has to be relevant to your audience. If you're building race cars, you won't get far talking about trunk size. Why? Because race car enthusiasts don't care about trunk size. (Also, I'm pretty sure race cars don't have trunks.) But if you're building family sedans, a story about trunk size, while not inherently interesting, is relevant to your potential customers.

It's remarkable how few business owners really grasp this. I know because, as I've mentioned before, I am occasionally approached by smart, successful CEOs and brand managers who want to start a word of mouth campaign about their company's anniversary or some other internal milestone. Not many people are going to talk about those things because they are relevant only to you and your employees. For a story to get passed around, it has to be somehow connected to the lives of the people doing the talking.

Interesting

A story has to be interesting so an influencer will pick it up and investigate it. There are all sorts of reasons that people may find a story interesting. But there are two particularly worth mentioning.

As C+C Music Factory showed us back in 1990, people love "Things that Make You Go Hmmm." Some stories simply make you stop what you're doing and consider them for a moment. Why? When you break it down, the "hmmm" factor can really be attributed to one thing: cognitive dissonance. Something challenges your assumptions, or it presents information in a way that doesn't immediately make sense to you, and you find yourself going, "Hmmm, interesting." For instance, shoppers in a mall see a uniformed person throwing toys and pine needles on the floor. They are going to stop and investigate that. (That anecdote will make more sense in a minute.)

People also pay attention to news—that is, information that is new or noteworthy to them, particularly about recent or important events. News is something you didn't know regarding a topic that interests you or that affects you directly. If you can present people with real news, they will stop and pay attention.

Authentic

Authentic stories are, by definition, true. But being authentic requires more than just telling the truth. "True" is the province of lawyers and public relations professionals. But for everyday people, it's easy to spot the difference between a story that is merely true and one that is authentic.

When it comes to marketing, an authentic story about your brand or category is one that matches what I as a consumer think I already know about it. When we were promoting PBR, we did not try to convince people it tasted like champagne because no one would have bought it (the story or the beer). In that same vein, we never would have suggested that Crocs be worn as eveningwear. Influencers will reject your story outright if it smells artificial.

One of the reasons Martha Stewart is so successful—and so talked about—is that people sense that she really does decorate pinecones for her Christmas dinner table and that she turns doilies into durable baby clothes in her spare time. Those "tips" from any other source wouldn't gain nearly as much traction. But Martha gets away with offering the most seemingly insane lifestyle advice because people can sense that is how she actually lives.

A good, talkable story is an authentic one. It's real. If country musician Zac Brown tried to sell a line of sushi mats, he would be stuck with a warehouse full of them. And no influencer would be caught dead talking about them to his friends who love country music (see the nearby Pro Tip). But tell a story that is true to who you are and what people know about you, and it will resonate. That kind of authenticity is key to talkability.

PRO TIP

Be authentic in your merchandising.

Like most touring musical groups, the Zac Brown Band used to conduct nightly meet-and-greets. Most bands use these moments to pose for pictures with a select group of fans— contest winners, friends of the crew, fan club members, and others—before their concerts. These gatherings are fun for the fans, but they can be fairly tedious for the bands. After all, the band members don't really get to interact much with the fans, and the event takes time away from activities that will actually help them prepare for the show, like eating dinner.

A few years ago, Zac Brown had an idea. Why not throw a big dinner party for everyone before the show: a fun and relaxed gathering where fans can get to know the band over good food. Instead of meet-and-greets, the band called them Eat-and-Greets.

Being a longtime barbecue fanatic, Zac hired an old friend, Rusty Hamlin who was an up-and-coming barbecue chef from Georgia, to handle the food. Rusty would travel with the band in his mobile kitchen, nicknamed Cookie, and prepare huge, locally sourced barbecue meals before every show—usually with Zac's help. For $50, fan club members could come and eat dinner with the band and hang out before the show.

Naturally, fans who experienced this couldn't wait to tell other fans about it. Stories of the Eat-and-Greets made their way onto Zac Brown forums and fan sites. *Fast Company* published an admiring article about Hamlin and the events. Before long, Zac developed a reputation for really knowing his barbecue—something he shared with his core audience of country music fans.

Today fans can buy Zac's Southern Ground Grub Brown Sauce, or his dry rub, or his pot apron. If the band had tried to sell these items before the Eat-and-Greets, it would have felt like a sham, a crass marketing ploy. But now, fans feel they are buying a little of the Zac Brown experience. It is just another way of showing that they belong to the tribe.

The Brunch Test

Congratulations. Your story has cleared the first three hurdles. It is relevant, interesting, and authentic. Now, take it to brunch. Practice telling it to your preoccupied brunch companions. Literally practice telling them the story. How would you bring it up? What are the relevant points you'd tell first? What are the interesting tidbits you'd use to draw them in? Are they with you? If not, why not?

PRO TIP

Take your staff to brunch and role-play.

If thought experiments are not your thing, take your staff to brunch (or dinner) and do some role-playing. Assign a role to each person—the distracted parent of two fussy kids, the executive with the buzzing phone, the skeptical teenager. Then practice telling them your story.

The point is to nail down the words and phrases you will use when you tell your CMO that you want to try some word of mouth marketing. Before you can tackle questions of budget and ROI, you need to be able to convince him or her that this whole thing makes sense. We spend a lot of time on this at Fizz, and it's amazing what a huge difference it makes. I encourage you to try it. You'll be grateful you did.

Remember, you need to be tough on yourself with the Brunch Test. Invite people who aren't necessarily inclined to listen to your story. It needs to engage people who didn't show up that day eager to hear what you have to say.

If you can honestly see this audience taking an interest in your story, you just might have something talkable. The next step is to find the right real-world audience for it. If you want your story to be passed around by people, you need to find the right people. You need to find your audience.

PRO TIP

Sometimes it's better to say nothing.

What if you look at your company and don't find any authentic, interesting, relevant stories to tell? What if nothing about your brand at this particular moment is likely to spark word of mouth? What if, talkability-wise, your cupboard is bare?

It's easy: say nothing.

You cannot force word of mouth. You cannot make influencers, or anyone for that matter, talk about something that is irrelevant, boring, and contrived. What you can do is put out a bad story that backfires on your company, triggering conversations about how silly or desperate you seem. If you're lucky, people just won't say anything.

A well-known car manufacturer once came to my agency wanting to do a word of mouth campaign. The average age of its customers was in the late fifties, and the company executives wanted to bring that down a decade or two. Unfortunately, there was a very good reason young people weren't buying these cars. This company's idea of a cool story was power windows and antilock brakes. True, stories about these features would have been perfectly authentic. And they would have been relevant to nearly any driver—who doesn't

(continues)

want antilock brakes? But, oh man, did they fail the interesting test. Nobody in this day and age is starting a conversation about power windows with anyone. And sadly, that was the best story this company had to offer.

My advice to them was the same as my advice would be to anyone with such a problem: Instead of spending your money on advertising, spend it on R&D. Create something worth talking about. Create something to differentiate you from the competition that you can use to start a conversation. Then you have a chance to get people talking.

Don't try to put out a story about a product that simply isn't worth talking about. Nothing good will come of that.

WHO GIVES A FUCK?

It's a basic truth of storytelling: very few stories are interesting to everyone. The six (and counting) Fast and Furious movies have grossed a total of nearly a billion dollars in box office receipts worldwide. Yet there are millions of people you couldn't pay to sit through a moment of these films. For some people, fast cars, hot women, and loud music constitute a perfect night at the movies. For others, they constitute a nightmare. It's all about putting your material in front of the right people.

To find those people, ask yourself one simple question. Who really cares? Or as we say at Fizz, "Who gives a fuck?" Think about the story behind your brand or product, and ask yourself the question. When you have your answer, you will be on your way to finding your audience.

The use of the word "fuck" is important here. We aren't asking, "Really, who cares?" We're asking, "Who *really* cares?" A lot. It's OK to target people who have a passing interest in your brand or product. But it's far better to target those who are likely to be passionate about it. You know, those people who really give a fuck. They are much more likely to spread your story faster and further.

As I noted earlier, people today are better able than ever to group themselves according to interest. Whether in person or online, fans create communities around their passions, from muscle cars to spicy foods to rap music. Figure out who would be interested in your story, and you'll have a pretty good idea which community you should be talking to.

Your Communities

Sometimes, finding your audience is easy and obvious. Selling a killer new car wax formulated specifically for antique cars? Get yourself to a classic car show and strike up some conversations. Got some ultra-stretchy workout pants to sell? To the yoga studio! As we discussed, beer festivals were practically invented as a launchpad for craft beer word of mouth campaigns.

But often, the products and services we sell do not inspire authentic communities of passionate fans. Sometimes, you have to think a little harder about where to find your audience, the one that will take an interest in your product and feel compelled to spread the word about it.

Brooms and vacuum cleaners fall firmly into this category. A few years ago, BISSELL hired our agency to spread the word about the BISSELL sweeper, a manual sweeper whose sales had been languishing. Communities of vacuum cleaner enthusiasts are, shall we say, thin on the ground. There are no vacuum cleaner parties to attend, no thriving online communities of vacuum enthusiasts. We needed a slightly more creative way to reach a community of people who would feel compelled to share the news about this new product.

And there was good reason to talk about it. This sweeper had a remarkable capacity for sweeping up small items usually left behind by vacuums and lesser sweepers—think tiny action figure accessories (swords, helmets, and so on), kitty litter, pine needles, and Lego blocks. If you have kids of a certain age, you know how annoying it is to step on Lego blocks. Plus, retrieving those pieces from the sweeper was far easier than retrieving them from the murky depths of a vacuum cleaner bag. Also, this cleaner didn't have a motor, making it far quieter than any vacuum.

We knew we had to get this sweeper in front of moms with young children. For one thing, years of research told us that moms make most of the household decisions regarding cleaning products. And young kids are most likely to have toys with lots of tiny pieces. They also take naps, which is when moms tended to clean—as quietly as possible.

Lucky for us, it was Christmastime, and moms everywhere were waging war on the pine needles falling off their Christmas trees. (Bonus: January is the biggest month for vacuum cleaner sales.) But where to demonstrate how effective the BISSELL sweeper was against this menace? Christmas tree farms? Too far, and not really a great environment for the sweepers. Next to the guys who sell trees on the sidewalks? Not a great place to do demonstrations; what if it rains?

Then we thought, what about the Santa line? Santa sits in a chair at the mall, and the kids stand in a slow-moving line with their parents next to a velvet rope. And there is never anything on the other side of that velvet rope, is there? What if we threw a bunch of pine needles and toys on a carpet on the other side of that rope and staged demonstrations?

So that's what we did, and it was a huge success. We had people wearing BISSELL shirts throwing all sorts of junk on a carpet from bags labeled "mess," and then showing what the sweeper could do. The moms were intrigued, but the kids were fascinated. "Mommy, that lady is making a mess!" they'd cry. "Can I help?" And we ended up with dozens of kids throwing toys and pine needles on the floor, who would then take turns helping our brand ambassadors scoop them up with the sweeper. You'd have thought they were playing with the hottest new toy of the season. (I actually have pictures of kids crossing off items on their Christmas list so they could add the sweeper. I would have loved to see Santa's face when he heard that request.)

You can probably guess what happened next. Moms whipped out their cell phone cameras and started snapping away. Their kids were already dolled up and coiffed to meet Santa, and now they were jostling over who would get to help the nice lady use the sweeper. Naturally, the moms posted these pictures of their kids on Facebook, Twitter, and Instagram. Thus, word spread, in the most adorable way possible, to thousands upon thousands of moms.

That was a talkable story. Right place, right time, right audience, authentic. And of course, as the kids were playing, moms were asking questions about the sweepers.

In the five years previous to our campaign, sales of that sweeper had been flat, and the five years previous to that, they had been declining. In the first year of our campaign, sales went up 15 percent. In the second year, they went up 25 percent.

Our campaign worked because we figured out who our audience was—who would want to talk about this product—and where to find these people. It didn't matter that they never congregated specifically to talk about vacuum cleaners. But they still existed as an authentic community of passionate consumers. We just had to figure out who they were, where to find them, and how to get their attention. That is the kind of storytelling that gets people talking.

PRO TIP

Look for people who are standing in line.

Whenever there is a line, there is an opportunity for a conversation. People in line are bored and will talk to anyone.

Plus, they are probably in a buying state of mind. If you can match your story to the interests of people in that line, you have a great starting point for a word of mouth campaign.

Grading Your Communities

Not all communities are created equal. Before you waste your time talking to a community that won't help spread your story, you need to evaluate and grade them. To do so, rate them on four criteria.

Strength of Communication

The strength of a group's communication is determined by the strength of the bonds between its members. Parents in a PTA will have strong bonds because their kids' education is at stake. Union members maintain very strong bonds because their rights, livelihood, and healthcare are on the line. Veterans' groups have strong bonds because they've been through wars together.

But plenty of people bring that same passion and urgency to their tennis club, or their Miley Cyrus fan club, because they, too, feel their very lives are at stake. When grading a community, look for signs that its members maintain tight bonds with one another, that they are passionate enough to hungrily consume and pass on any relevant information about the topic at hand. You want to be dealing with groups that communicate frequently and efficiently. Word of mouth doesn't work if people aren't talking to one another.

In 2012, Fizz was helping a giant U.S.-based telcom spread the word about its 4G LTE mobile Internet connection. The goal was to move customers from 4G, which had become crowded and sluggish, to 4G LTE, which was new and moved at lightning speeds. Moving customers out of gridlock and into the fast lane would benefit the customers, but it would also save the company money.

Our first job was to find communities that would care deeply about faster Internet speeds. One of the more surprising groups we came up with was hairstylists. Why hairstylists? For one, hairstylists as a community are very strong communicators.

Throughout their careers, typical stylists will work at dozens of different salons. They get to know a lot of different hairstylists, and they maintain vast, complex networks of colleagues and references. They are also a talkative bunch who love to share professional tips and news with one another. So when hairstylists spread the news, they aren't just talking to the guy one chair over. They're talking to their coworkers from two, three salons ago. It's kind of a never-ending, citywide hairstylist conversation.

Photos are very important to hairstylists too. There are two reasons for this: One, because they change salons so often, smart stylists maintain a "lookbook" with photos of all their best hairdos. It's basically a portfolio of their work. Of course, styles change quickly, so the stylists are constantly updating these lookbooks. The easier it is to shoot and upload high-quality pictures, the easier it is for them to maintain their book.

Two, stylists are frequently asked to re-create a hairstyle from the pages of a magazine. Customers tear out pictures of their favorite celebrity hairdos and ask stylists to replicate the look on them. But for the stylists, this can be a problem. For one, a single picture of a hairdo doesn't necessarily contain enough information—What does it look like from the back? Or the top?—for the stylists to work with. And then there is the problem of color, as we found with women who wanted to look like the singer Katy Perry.

After Katy Perry divorced Russell Brand in late 2012, she dyed her hair an electric shade of blue—a small act of feminine defiance that resonated with a lot of women. Soon, customers were walking into salons holding pictures of Katy Perry, saying they wanted exactly that shade of blue.

Unfortunately, magazine pictures are not great when it comes to capturing true colors. Perry's blue hair in *People* didn't quite match her blue hair in *Us Weekly*. So these women walking in with

the magazine clippings all risked walking out with slightly different color hair than they really wanted.

We gave a bunch of hairstylists 4G LTE tablets to use for a couple of weeks. Now, when a customer asked for Katy Perry Blue, the
stylist could simply Google it and find hundreds of pictures in an
instant. If someone wanted Jennifer Aniston's haircut, the stylist
didn't have to ask, "Which one?" She could just search online—
again, superfast—for the pictures. The speedy tablets also helped
the stylists cut down on the time they spent uploading and editing
photos for their lookbooks.

Word spread quickly among the stylists that this tool could
both save them time and make their customers happy. Before we
knew it, salon owners were coming to us saying they had heard
about these tablets, and they wanted them for their own store.
Those owners were so pleased that they equipped their whole
shops with 4G LTE. Our client, of course, was pleased too. That was
a great example of a tight-knit community quickly spreading the
word about a relevant product.

But hairstylists don't talk exclusively to hairstylists, of course.
One other thing we knew about stylists from the beginning was
that their customers put a lot of trust in them. In surveys where
women are asked to name the people they trust most, time and
again they name their husband first and their hairstylist second.
So when these women saw their stylists using the 4G LTE tablets,
they took that as a very easy and natural recommendation from a
trusted source.

These hairstylists were not only good at telling each other
about 4G LTE but they were also good at spreading the word to the
larger consumer community. That's an example of really strong

communicators, even though hairstylists may not be the first group you think of when you hear "community."

Speed of Communication

Flight attendants talk to each other during takeoffs or landings, or between beverage services. Bartenders talk to waiters having a drink after their shifts end. People in groups like these will spread information faster than those who need to go out of their way to find time to talk to one another.

When looking at a community, ask yourself, How practiced are these people at sharing stories with one another? Are there established routines among them for passing on information? Think about every cop show you've ever seen, when the captain stands in front of the force each morning and runs down the list of the day's threats. Or nurses passing on patient information at the end of their shifts. These routines ensure that information will be passed on in a timely manner.

When thinking about this, it's important to be open-minded. Not all established routines look like established routines. Once, a client of ours that made a platform for mobile payments wanted to reach out to vendors who needed to be mobile. We eventually settled on artists and craftspeople who were selling their goods at traveling street fairs. These folks were spending hour upon hour sitting in their booths as browsers came and went. And as they sat there, they would naturally talk to the guy in the next booth over, sharing stories, news, and gossip. It wasn't quite morning announcements, but it had the same effect: information spread quickly among these folks because there was an established, recurring method of communication.

Age of the Community

A community with an Internet forum that nobody visits is not really a community. So ask yourself, How well established is this community? Do its members meet once a month? Do they talk daily? Or do they share stories only when they see each other at conventions once a year? You want to work with communities that have a reason to exist beyond you. You want people who are showing up as often as they can because the more they show up, the more they will share stories.

Word of mouth is ultimately a numbers game—you need a lot of people to share your story, so a lot of other people will buy your stuff. It matters that these people truly exist as a community in spirit as well as name.

Authenticity

Members of an authentic community are there because they love the topic and they want to be around others who share their passion. An authentic community consists of people who would lose or spend money to be part of it if they had to. The more that members of a community are being compensated, the less authentic the community.

One of the most authentic communities I have ever seen is around the video game *Civilization* by Sid Meier. It's a complicated game with a dedicated following. This particular online message board was started by a guy who worked for the Coast Guard and lived in Alaska. This guy had no connection to the company that manufactured the game, and he wasn't, as far as I know, a professional gamer in any sense. But he was passionate about this game, so in his spare time, he moderated this board.

At first, people visited this message board to get tips and help for playing the game (as I said, it's complicated). But as time went on, the board attracted so much attention from *Civilization* fans that it became a base for organizing meetups and tournaments. It evolved into the de facto *Civilization* clubhouse—all because people were attracted to the proprietor's very real love of the game. Other players could sense that he took it as seriously, if not more so, than they did, and they knew that he was in it for the pure love of it and not any kind of compensation. It was an authentic community, and that attracted more and more people with a real interest in the topic.

That is just one example of an authentic community. The question is, How do we as brands and companies achieve the same thing on a regular basis?

Starting Your Own Community

If there is no existing authentic community around your topic or brand, you can create one. You just have to be careful about how you do it. It is completely OK to say to people, "We think what we're doing is awesome." The trick is to do it in such a way that you attract people who aren't necessarily looking to be compensated for their involvement. Offer $5 off the next purchase for anyone who likes your Facebook page and you will quickly amass a "community." But these are worthless connections because these people do not care about your brand. They care about saving money.

Craft brewers are masters at this. Read the side of a small-batch beer bottle sometime. Most craft brewers really, truly love their own beer, and that enthusiasm comes across when they describe their ingredients and brewing process. "Our beer is awesome, and this is how we made it that way."

Here are four good rules to follow when starting a community around your brand.

Share Almost Everything

You have to be honest, but not exhaustively so. Under no circumstances should you lie, but that doesn't mean you have to divulge every detail either. Think of your community kind of like your ex. You can talk about yourself without oversharing. But you do need to be fundamentally transparent.

If your community starts asking questions about something you'd rather not talk about, you have to be prepared to discuss it. But that doesn't mean you need to foster conversations about your secrets.

Listen to Everyone

If you're going to invite people to share their stories and feelings about your brand with you and each other, you have to listen to everyone. You cannot simply ignore some people because you do not like what they have to say.

You're throwing the party, you're sending out the invitations, and you have to treat all your guests with respect.

Celebrate the Ideas You Love

That doesn't mean you have to celebrate every comment equally. The nice part about hosting your own community is you get to pick and choose to whom you're going to show the most love.

Blogs such as *Deadspin* and even large publications like the *New York Times* have comment sections that allow anyone and everyone to weigh in. But the brands themselves (and the readers, to an extent) control which comments get highlighted. This is instructive for any brand-run community. Let everyone have his or her say, but don't feel obligated to celebrate every comment— or commenter—equally.

Don't Fake It

Simply put, there is nothing wrong with simply showing your customers that you are as enthusiastic about your product as they are.

Of course, you genuinely need to be enthusiastic about it. It's hard to fake being psyched about, say, antilock brakes and power windows. If you aren't excited about your own product, you have problems that word of mouth marketing can't solve.

- - - - - - - - - -

Now that you've found and graded your communities, the next step is to figure out where they live.

PRO TIP

Create an authentic community.

Maker's Mark has done an amazing job creating an authentic community around its own brand with its Ambassadors program. On the surface, the program is not all that different from your average fan club. By signing up, Maker's Mark fans get plenty of perks—like first peeks at new bottles or first opportunities to buy new products. But the difference in its approach is its spirit of openness and free exchange, nicely illustrated by a minor fiasco from February 2013.

At that time, Maker's Mark found itself in a tough position. In order to meet growing demand amid dwindling supply, it had made the decision to water down its bourbon. Knowing the public probably wouldn't love the idea, the company first broke the news by e-mailing everyone in its Ambassador program. The idea was to get early buy-in from its most passionate customers. They didn't try to hide it or couch it in fancy PR-speak. The company came right out and leveled with its fans.

Not surprisingly, the fans didn't take it well. The Ambassadors flooded social media with their anger over the move, and the media swarmed all over the story. Within weeks, Maker's Mark had reversed the decision, saying it would risk selling fewer bottles if the fans were willing to pay a little more for the product. When announcing the decision, the company once again e-mailed the Ambassadors first.

The result? The company's biggest fans felt closer to each other and the company. They felt that Maker's Mark cared about their opinion and were willing to make changes to keep them happy. At the end of the day, the community was reminded of its strength, and the whole program was imbued with a sense of authenticity. That's head and shoulders above your usual fan club. The message behind the entire Maker's Mark Ambassador program is: You're into bourbon. We're into bourbon. Let's be into bourbon together.

TAKING ADVANTAGE OF
THE AMPLIFICATION PRINCIPLE

Why do we talk to small communities? Because by talking to small communities, we can eventually talk to everyone who cares about a particular subject, even if they do not belong or they have never heard of these communities.

You Don't Have to Build Every
Part of the Mousetrap

This is a principle at the heart of word of mouth marketing. You can't personally share your story with everyone, and you don't necessarily want to. You want to find the people who will care the most about your story, who know and are able to influence the most other people who will care about your story, and who have the deepest internal motivation for sharing it.

How does a story spread? Give moms a great story to tell about your sweeper: "We were waiting in line to see Santa, and there was this woman with a bag labeled 'mess' throwing action figures and pine needles all over a carpet. Zach ran up and asked if he could use the sweeper too, and next thing you know, he is sweeping up toys in the middle of the mall. By the way, you should check out this sweeper because it really did seem to suck up the pine needles."

All you need is one of these moms standing around the playground to tell two friends this story. Then those friends will tell two friends, and so on. Armed with this story, the right mom can infect an entire school. And if you win the school, you win the neighborhood. Win the neighborhood, and you can win the state. And so on and so on.

Here's a confession: We never thought about the parents' cell phones in the Santa line during the BISSELL sweeper program. We missed that as a potential communications channel. Should we have anticipated it? Absolutely. But we were thinking about conversations, and to be sure, we started many. We simply didn't consider the potential visual aspect of what we were presenting—well-dressed kids playing with a sweeper in the middle of a mall—until we saw the cell phones come out. We were focused on telling the right story to the right people at the right time, trusting that at least 1 out of every 10 of them would have that influencer personality.

Because we got those elements right, we didn't need to worry about the cell phones. Frankly, we also weren't worrying about whether these moms would tell their friends about the sweeper while they were at the playground or while they were picking up their kids from school or while they were at a cocktail party. It's just about putting yourself in the right position. It's about finding communities, figuring out where they gather—virtually or in person—and perfecting the story you put in front of them. At least 1 out of 10 of them will take care of the rest. It's also about training your people correctly. If you've done that, you don't have to worry about your ambassadors' capacity to adapt to unforeseen circumstances. With the proper training, when your ambassadors see something in the field, they will be able to take advantage of it. The day after we saw the phones come out, we sent a notice to everyone to think about the phones. This was not a tough adjustment to make because we had trained everyone well.

You don't have to worry about building the whole mousetrap. This is one reason we tell our stories to preexisting communities. They build the mousetrap for us. It's all in their desire to share the story.

Don't Be Annoying

You know who won't share your stories? People who think you are annoying. And when you are trying to start conversations with strangers in public places, you always run the risk of annoying them.

They say you should never come up with a negative rule in marketing. Well, here are two: Never interrupt someone. Never annoy someone.

Here are the two worst things you can do in marketing, as far as I'm concerned:

1. Call someone during dinner time.

2. Spray something on people in the mall.

No one goes to the mall to get sprayed, and absolutely no one sits down to dinner hoping a stranger with something to sell will dial his number at that moment. If your objective is to start a conversation with someone, and you start by getting in the way of something else he was trying to do, that's bad. Who wants to start a conversation with an annoying person?

Again, give yourself the Brunch Test. If your best friend and your mother-in-law are in the middle of a conversation, and you interrupt them mid-dialogue to tell them a story about something utterly unrelated to what they were talking about, are they going to be interested? Or will you have turned them off from the get-go?

No, starting a solid conversation with someone frequently means letting them come to you. Like those kids and the sweepers—we didn't push a BISSELL in anyone's face. We weren't annoying about it. We put our product in front of the right people at the right time, and conversations happened. Sometimes it's hard to strike up a conversation without being intrusive. But you can always find a way.

Put Your Story to the Test

People sometimes dismiss word of mouth marketing because they don't understand it. They think the idea is to tell 10 random people about a product, who will each then tell 2 people, and so on and so on, until the world knows about it and decides to buy it. What those people don't appreciate is that these communities exist—these deep, robust networks of influencers who are already talking to their friends and colleagues about their passions, which often include brands and products. All you're doing is giving them something new to talk about. You're feeding the beast, not giving birth to it. Talk to the right people in the right community about the right story, and it will spread as far as any commercial message—and with far more force.

But to know if that story is right, you have to test it. Yes, you can go out and spend $300,000 on A/B testing and focus groups. Or you can do the simple tests outlined in this chapter. Ask yourself, Who wants to hear this story? And under what conditions?

Is this a story that will inspire more conversations? Is it something people—even those who aren't inclined to trust you—will want to talk about? If so, who are these people and where do you find them?

If every answer is yes, then go for it. You may have a talkable story. If not, change your story. Because these days, when loved ones and influencers hold far more sway over our purchasing decisions than any other factor, it is becoming harder and harder to sell a brand that people don't care to talk about.

CHAPTER 4

Strategic Corporals: How and Why to Train Your Brand Ambassadors

If you're going to get people talking, you have to get out there and start talking to people. For this, you're going to need help.

That means you will have to choose and train *brand ambassadors*. These are the folks who will be introducing potential customers to your brand and its story. They are enormously important, so you need to train them well. Specifically, you need to train them like Marines, not Sailors.

Am I putting down the Navy? Not a chance. The way the Navy trains its people is just very different from how the Marines do it. When it comes to word of mouth marketing, too many people train their brand ambassadors in the Navy style. What you need are Marines.

THE THREE BLOCK WAR

In the 1990s, the Marines found themselves spending less and less time on a conventional battlefield. (Sound familiar?) Instead of fighting the occasional full-scale conflict like Word War II,

Marines were now intervening in small regional conflicts like those in Haiti or Mogadishu, seemingly once a month.

In fact, between 1990 and 1999, the Corps responded to an average of one crisis every five weeks—three times the rate of the Cold War.[1]

These new kinds of engagements required a new kind of Marine. Because these were not full-on wars and because they often occurred in dense, urban environments that blurred the line between combatant and bystander, a Marine needed a broad range of skills to succeed. On one block he may need to launch mortars, but on the next he may need to shelter refugees, and on the next block he may need to corral a swarming media. A good Marine would need the skills to handle all three situations.

General Charles C. Krulak, then commandant of the Corps, gave this new kind of conflict a name. He called it the Three Block War.[2]

In a Three Block War, you could not have one guy who knew only how to rewire hospital electricity and another guy who knew only how to drive the tank. Everyone had to know how do to every job.

Another hallmark of the Three Block Wars was chaos. They tended to escalate quickly and change unpredictably. Thus each Marine would have to be trusted to act independently if the need arose. He had to make good decisions on the fly, even when his commanding officer was not reachable. As we saw in Mogadishu, in the infamous "Black Hawk Down" battle, the actions of a single Marine could affect the entire mission and have serious geopolitical repercussions. This meant that even low-level commanders needed enough operational knowledge to make decisions that the Corps could later defend to Congress and the media.

To succeed in such an environment, every Marine had to become a "strategic corporal," said General Krulak, and he had to be someone who could make big decisions and execute them, regardless of his rank.

This is very different from Navy training. Ships are like factories, in which every person must receive extensive training to perform a specific job. It is unrealistic to expect every person on an aircraft carrier to be able to perform every job. Instead, each person becomes an expert in his or her narrow set of tasks, and everyone works together.

The problem with too many companies is that they treat their brand ambassadors as if they were in the Navy. They assign them one job to do efficiently, like pass out samples or take pictures. And they neither allow nor train their ambassadors to do anything else.

In our modern marketing world of chaos and consumer information saturation, what they need are strategic corporals.

Your Brand Ambassadors

Brand ambassadors are the men and women who venture forth to share your story in the commercial jungles of America (speaking of dense, chaotic environments where conflict can escalate quickly). These people hold enormous power to sway opinion about your brand.

It's really important that you choose and train these people well.

This was not always so. In a world of broadcast, the guy you hired to hand out flyers at the car show wasn't really affecting anyone's opinion of your brand. He didn't need to know much about your company. But in a world driven by conversation, that person may represent the first interaction with your brand that many people have. If your brand is a tribe, your ambassador is the rush chairman for that tribe. A person's decision to join—that is, buy your product—could hinge greatly on his feelings about this person.

The environment into which you will be dropping these people is unpredictable, and the results are very important to you and your company. Think about the man we sent to the mall to talk about how well BISSELL sweepers sucked up pine needles. His potential audience was anyone in that mall with a live Christmas tree at home. This included moms, dads, cat owners, dog owners, smokers, people with allergies, people who love their carpets, grandparents, and nearly everyone else.

These are all very different groups of people, and they will all have different questions about the product. They don't care that your company has one message it is trying to convey. In fact, here's a guy asking a totally irrelevant question. And here comes another with a very boring story he wants to tell you. Oh and look, that kid is trying to use your samples. And apparently, the wife of the man you're talking to is convinced she knows more about this subject than you do. Your brand ambassador must be able to get that message across to everyone, to make it relevant to anyone's life, despite constant distractions amid the worst of conditions.

Too many brand ambassador programs today don't give their trainees the tools to operate independently. Instead of training them to be smart, empowered advocates who can talk passionately and extemporaneously about the brand, they teach their brand ambassadors to do two things and two things only: stick to the script, and bring back something to measure. Fear is the reason that marketers focus on these things, and it often ruins their outreach efforts.

Stick to the Script

Do not try to control from your office what a brand ambassador does in public. Understandably, it terrifies many executives to have low-level employees or volunteers interacting with the public on their company's behalf. So they give their ambassadors carefully worded, lawyer-approved scripts with six or seven easy-to-remember talking points that they are told never to stray from.

So what is supposed to happen when these ambassadors, the people you entrusted with your brand's image, are asked a tough question from a genuinely interested party? Smile and act like they didn't hear it? By asking people to stick to the script, you are sending soldiers into battle with only one weapon.

If you're going to send people out into the field, you need to give them the tools and the knowledge to succeed. You need to tell them everything about your brand, not just the things you wish people would talk about.

Bring Me Something to Measure

As is true in every other marketing program, CMOs have to justify the money they spend on word of mouth marketing. They have to find a way to measure the impact these people are having, so the procurement department will continue to sign the checks. But measuring word of mouth marketing—particularly the value of a single group of brand ambassadors—is extremely challenging.

How do you measure the dollar value of a conversation? So field marketers have come up with dozens of metrics that can be measured—arrival time, departure time, number of samples distributed, number of e-mail addresses collected. Throw enough of these numbers on a PowerPoint presentation, and after a while, they start to look like results.

The problem is that nothing listed above will have anywhere near as big an impact on your brand as a single enlightened conversation with a passionate fan.

Eventually, these superficial "objectives" become the whole focus of your program. Who can give out the most sweatshirts? Who stays at the event the longest? Who gets the most guys to pose with them for pictures? In turn, that affects the kind of people you hire. Instead of good brand representatives, you end up with a small army of very punctual, sample-distributing people whose job it is to perform a limited set of tasks and not get into trouble.

But nothing they are tasked to do will ever get a real conversation going. Instead, they are afraid to have real conversations because it might knock them "off message." None of them can get you tapped into an influencer's network. None of them are getting anyone to buy your product.

Your sole objective for all outreach in the community should be to identify influencers and tell them a story they can share with friends. This is much harder to measure. But it does actually work. These are the things that will advance your ultimate goal, which is to sell more stuff to more people more often for more money.

PRO TIP

Remember the two rules of swag.

A quick word about swag. No one goes to a bar to get a free branded shot glass. They go to watch the game, meet friends, maybe get drunk. They don't go to NASCAR events to get a free hat emblazoned with the name of a cell phone provider.

Handing out swag too often becomes a marketing objective because it's easy to measure. And that's a terrible reason to focus on anything. Trust me, you do not want your word of mouth marketing program to devolve into a giant swag party.

But swag can be powerful if it doesn't suck. So remember Fizz's two rules of swag:

1. It must be of high quality in terms of design, material, or cultural resonance.

2. It should never be used as a substitute for conversation. Hand it out only as an afterthought, not as your prime reason for being there.

Follow those two rules and you'll see your swag get worn, shared, and shown off among your target audience members. We've got the PBR hats to prove it.

FINDING YOUR AMBASSADORS

Before you can train your brand ambassadors, you need to find them. It's important you get the right people because as good and rigorous as your training may be, there are some things you cannot teach.

Good brand ambassadors possess most of the influencer personality traits, which (again) are these:

1. They are interested in new things because they are new.

2. They share stories with their friends.

3. They are intrinsically motivated.

You cannot teach someone to be an influencer. But you can learn to recognize one when you see her.

A good brand ambassador is passionate. Ideally, she is already passionate about your brand, but barring that, she should have real passion about your kind of product in general. You cannot fake the kind of passion a sneakerhead has for Air Jordans or the passion a home chef has for his Viking range. Your ambassadors have to really want to get out there and tell people about your brand. They have to love talking about this stuff.

Where to Look

So where do you go to find these people?

Craigslist

Yes, the same website you used to sell your old couch for $15 can also help you find some fantastic brand ambassadors. As it turns out, the ambassadors who do it a lot—particularly junior and mid-level ones—use Craigslist to find most of their jobs. (Once these folks become senior enough, they usually have a network of employers to keep them busy, but they will still troll Craigslist now and then in search of new opportunities.)

To me, it seems strange that nobody has come up with a better way, but the truth is, the site is a great place to find solid employees who will stay with you for months or years at a time. So don't be afraid to take advantage of it.

Internet Forums

You will never find a more passionate group of people than those who frequent Internet forums. If you're looking for people who would love to stand around all day talking about their hobby, Internet forums are a great place to start.

Be warned: When it comes to distrusting outsiders, the Amish have nothing on people who post online about tequila all day. If you're going to operate in these forums, you need to prove your worth. You do that by being utterly transparent and 100 percent authentic.

Start by going to the leaders—a.k.a. the "admins"—and paying your respects. Do not just wander into the forum, choose some silly username, and start a thread soliciting brand ambassadors. Most of the time, that will just get you ejected from the site like a foreign antibody. Instead, go to the admins and say, "This is who we are, and this is what we are doing. Go ahead and check us out." Then tell them about the people you are looking for—men between the ages of 18 and 25 who are really into stamp collecting, for example. Odds are, the admins will know of someone who fits your description, and most of the time, they will be happy to hook you up.

If instead the admins tell you to get out, then do us all a favor and get out. Maybe the folks on this forum have been burned by marketing people before. Maybe they're just not interested. Either way, there is no use trying to argue with them. And there is always another forum.

In fact, most forums have a *rival* forum, and you can use this to your advantage. If one forum is giving you the cold shoulder, go to its rival and say, "Hey, the guys in that other forum told me to get out. But maybe you can help us out. We're looking for some *real* stamp collectors."

Conventions, Concerts, Parades, and Festivals

If you make the world's best earbuds, go to a concert. If you're making knitting needles, go to a craft fair. If you make music, the RIAA has created the Record Store Day.

In-person events are a great place to find volunteers who clearly care enough about a particular topic to leave their house for it. And they offer the added benefit of face-to-face meetings, where you can get a sense of just how much of an influencer personality a potential ambassador might have.

To Compensate or Not?

Are you going to pay your brand ambassadors? Well, that is a perfectly fine thing to do, if you are so inclined. But ask yourself a few things first.

How many paid staff do you think work at the Masters Golf Tournament every year? Out of the hundreds of people working the grounds that day, about 65 are actually paid. The rest do it just because they love the game. Maybe they can't afford tickets but they want to see it from up close. Maybe they're just hoping for a behind-the-scenes peek at their favorite golfers.

How many people do you think get paid to work at Comic-Con? Or Fashion Week? People practically trip over themselves to volunteer for events like these. It gives them standing in their niche community, special access, and great stories to share. So what if they have to work a little? They would pay to be there if they had to.

The point is, you may be surprised at how willing some people are to work without pay for a brand or category they love. Granted, not every client has an experience like Comic-Con or the Masters to offer. So you may have to offer some compensation. But it does not have to be much—and really, it shouldn't be. For one thing, most of the people you will be working with already have jobs (not many people think of brand ambassador as a career path). The work they're doing with you is what they would be doing if they didn't have to work.

You also don't want to pay so much that people are incentivized to fake their enthusiasm for your brand. You don't want people talking about your brand strictly for the money. Ideally, your brand ambassadors would be talking about your brand anyway; you're just paying them to talk about it a lot more (and for their time and professionalism). The last thing you want is someone faking it to cash a check.

If you are going to pay your ambassadors, pay them a living wage, and insist they be 100 percent transparent about it. There is never any reason a brand ambassador should lie about being paid. Some people get nervous that potential customers will be turned off if they find out the guy talking to them so enthusiastically about a product is being paid. But in my experience, if you have hired solid influencers who are talking to people who they know share their passion, that is never a problem. In fact, the conversation usually goes like this:

> **New friend:** Dude, why do you know so much about these sneakers?
>
> **Brand ambassador:** This is my job. I get paid to talk to people about cool sneakers.

New friend: You're serious? You get paid to talk about sneakers?

Brand ambassador: Yep.

New friend: Wow. How do I get that job?

This is just one more reason why, in a world driven by conversation, brand ambassadors must be passionate about your product before you can pay them. A guy who travels the country talking about antilock brakes and slip differential with a bunch of gear heads isn't just doing it for the money. Such a conversation would never be authentic if the brand ambassador weren't also an influencer and didn't love cars. You can't fake passion for a brand, and you really don't want your brand ambassadors to have to try to. You have to give influencers a reason to want to talk about your stuff.

PRO TIP

Don't fall into the trap of casting someone based on a certain look.

You should be hiring for passion and the ability to have a conversation.

In a broadcast world, it makes sense to favor looks over personality. Commercials are tightly scripted and rely heavily on visuals, so what does it matter whether the actor actually cares about your brand?

In a word of mouth world, you want someone who can share your message, who can get it out there no matter what is happening around him. What he looks like doesn't particularly matter. In fact, working against type can be a benefit to your brand. If the person talking to me about the Atlanta Hawks doesn't fit my preconceived notion of what a basketball fan should look like, then I may just have to reconsider my preconceived notions. Maybe I don't know everything about this brand I thought I did.

By that same token, there is nothing worse than a brand ambassador who fits my preconceived notions of your brand, yet can't hold an intelligent conversation. Now I have all the confirmation I need to write your brand off forever.

Casting to type is a very dangerous thing to do in word of mouth marketing. Avoid it at all costs.

Swag

One popular way to reward brand ambassadors is to load them up with swag. Hats, jerseys, bottle openers, jackets, whatever. I'll tell you this: No one ever became a brand ambassador, or volunteered at Fashion Week or the Masters, for the free bag of junk. No one is going to complain if you don't give them a hat with your logo on it. It's not necessary, so don't feel obligated to give it.

That said, if you are determined to give your people swag, please follow one basic rule. Don't be cheap! Nobody needs another travel mug. You don't have to give everyone a Rolex, but it should be something of value, something of high quality. If you can't afford that, just forget the swag. You don't want to work with the guy who's just there for the jacket anyway.

The Influencer Tests

Once you've found a group of potential ambassadors, you need to find out who among them is suited for the job. This means finding the people with influencer personalities. This is, as you can probably guess, not an exact science. But it is also easier than you think.

First, why do you need your brand ambassadors to have influencer personalities? For one thing, you want this to come naturally to them. Going out and talking to strangers about a product or brand isn't for everyone. To some, it would be a nightmare. But to most influencers, it's pretty easy. It's what they do naturally.

Influencers also tend to be good storytellers, and they're great at making their stories relevant to the people they're talking to. Influencers want to be listened to, so they've usually developed pretty good conversation skills. This is an important trait for brand ambassadors.

Luckily, influencers are fairly easy to identify. In fact, after a while, you just start to know one when you see one. And the fact is, once these applicants find out what the job is, and what it pays, there's not much incentive for a noninfluencer to stick around. Still, there are some tests you can run to be more certain.

A/B Testing

Offer your applicants a choice of gifts. One gift has some cash value; the other is an experience. The influencers will choose the experience every time.

For example, Choice A is a $250 gift card to AutoZone; Choice B is a two-lap ride on the Porsche test track. They may be tempted to take the cash value, but a real influencer with a passion for sports cars would never turn down an experience like that simulator.

He can already see himself telling his Porsche buddies about it. He can tell that story for years. That's the guy you want.

PRO TIP

Find out if the influencers will choose the experience instead of the gift.

Offering potential brand ambassadors a choice between gifts, one with cash value and one that's a talkable experience, works on the same principle as Zappos's famous offer to new recruits. After going through an intensive four-week training program, Zappos employees are offered $3,000 to quit. Take the money and run, no hard feelings. The point is to weed out anyone who, even after the training, is more tempted by money than the thrill of the work.

You might think at least half the recruits would take the cash. But Zappos claims that only about 3 percent do. That's 97 percent who say no to the money and stick around for the job.

This is what you want to do with your brand ambassadors. Make it easy for people who are more motivated by money than fun experiences and conversations to self-identify and show themselves the door. Real influencers will take the experience every time.

Conversational Interview

Valuing experience over money isn't enough. To do this job well, a brand ambassador has to be a natural storyteller. Sit down with her, and get her talking. Come up with questions that could prompt someone to share a story with you, and see how eagerly she takes the bait.

For example, ask her why she feels so passionately about the brand. Does she respond with a list of attributes? "Tastes great, less filling?" Or does she tell you about the first time she tasted it, the people she was with, and what the product has meant to her over the years? That's your storyteller.

The Pitch

This one will not only tell you if a person is a good storyteller but also if she can talk to you about the product in detail, if she can impart technical details cogently and coherently, and if she can do this without sounding stunted or programmed.

First, give the candidate some technical details about the product. Then tell her you'll be playing the role of the busy dad stuck in line at the grocery store, or the skeptical superfan at Comic-Con. She then has to talk to you about the product as if you are that person. You, of course, will try to throw her off. Judge it the way you would a beauty pageant: eloquence, poise, an ability to think quickly. All of these count.

The Grunt Work

The final test, which is far less interesting than the others but is just as important, is to see if they're willing and able to attend the weekly phone call meetings, prepare the PowerPoint report every week, or whatever it is the brand managers require of them. You don't want to make these things the focus of your program, but they are still important.

Your objectives should remain firmly focused on starting conversations with influencers, but you do need your ambassadors to share their experiences in the field with you. You need an idea of whom they spoke to and what sorts of responses they got, so you can make adjustments to your strategy. They should be your partners in spreading the word. Their feedback will be instrumental to refining your story and how you spread it. You need to make sure they are willing to handle some responsibility on that end.

That's why strategic corporals are hard to find and expensive to train. They are not circus animals handing out tchotchkes. They are a living part of your word of mouth program. You have to take the time and expense to train them right.

A KOBAYASHI MARU

When your brand ambassadors get out into the field, they are going to fail. Not every day, and not so badly that they can't recover, but they *will* fail. They will be rejected, ignored, harassed, scolded, laughed at, and generally disrespected at one point or another. This is tough for anyone to take. To prepare them for that, you need to get them comfortable with failure. You need to fail them before they go out into the world. That's why your training needs to include a Kobayashi Maru.

A Kobayashi Maru is an unpassable test used to gauge the character of the test taker. The point of the test is to see how the subject responds to failure, to see if he can adjust and move forward when things don't go according to plan.

If it turns out that they can't handle failure, then you really do need to send them home.

The next thing to know about training is that it takes longer than you think. However long you think you need to train your ambassadors, double it. We're not doing an afternoon in the conference room with two snack breaks here. At Fizz, we think training takes a solid week. If you're dealing with a technical product, it will probably take two.

Finally, you must be prepared to overshare. You must overshare information about the company and the brand and the product and the packaging and the manufacturing and the marketing and the CEO's first marriage if you have to. The more information these folks have, the easier it will be for them to craft stories that will be interesting to a wide range of people. Oversharing is how you create ambassadors who can carry on intelligent, informative conversations about your brand and not sound like bad actors in a poorly written play about marketing.

Structuring the Training

There are different ways to structure your training. And however you do it, most of your time is going to be spent teaching your ambassadors about the brand and testing their ability to talk about it under tough conditions.

Here's how we do it at Fizz.

Training Day 1

Our theme for Day 1 is How This Works, and What We Want to Accomplish. In the morning, we explain what word of mouth marketing is, what it isn't, and why it works. In the afternoon, we start to talk about the brand and our objective for the campaign.

Throughout the training, it's important to mix things up. A little lecturing is fine and unavoidable, but please, do not talk these people to death. For one, they are there to help you. Two, not everyone learns by sitting and listening. Different people learn in different ways. Your training has to be multidimensional enough to address everyone's needs.

We have had trainees make us collages to express their feelings about the brand. We have used coloring books and Legos. Make it as hands-on as you can.

Is there somewhere you can take your trainees to learn more about the brand? This is a great thing to do on Day 1. Take a field trip, hold a tasting, visit a manufacturing plant. Expose them to every dimension of the brand so that they will have the widest possible base of knowledge to use when crafting stories.

At some point during the day, we make a list of bad habits for brand ambassadors, and we explain why each habit is bad. This is the list of habits that you will beat out of your people for the next week, so you might as well get it on the table now. Trust me, whoever you're training, whether or not they've done field marketing work before, has picked up some bad ideas about passing out free stuff, about getting someone's attention, about talking to strangers on behalf of a brand. There is more to this job than making sure you pass out every cup in your trunk, and there is a way to do it without being obnoxious.

Some common bad habits:

1. Handing out stuff just for the sake of handing out stuff

2. Chasing people

3. Trying to have a conversation with every person who passes by

4. Being more concerned with the process (reports, arrival and departure times, number of hats distributed) than with having good conversations

Remember, people have gotten into these bad habits because brand managers have gotten into the habit of judging them on these things. They have been taught that it's more important to have a lot of conversations than a few good ones with the right people. You need to break them of these habits, not shame them for having picked them up.

That night, take them out and do something social. Have a little fun.

PRO TIP

Beware of professional brand ambassadors who have been at it too long.

If you do find yourself working with professional brand ambassadors, I recommend limiting it to people with more than two years' experience but less than five. It's good to be comfortable with the job, but the longer one does it, the more bad habits one picks up from other non–word of mouth projects.

Too many other field marketers have taught them that the job is all about staying the longest and giving out the most stuff. After a while, it becomes impossible to get these poor battered souls to focus on anything else.

Training Day 2

Today is all about practice. They should know a good bit about the brand now. Make them practice, practice, practice. Do some role-playing. Have them talk to you about the brand while you act interested, then not interested, then distracted, then creepily overinterested, then flat-out rude. Have them role-play with each other. Make it hard. Fail people. This is where you teach them to deal with rejection and profanity and whatever else the general public may throw at them.

And when I say "fail people," I do mean fail them. Tell them they aren't getting it, and make them do it again. If they really can't get it right, you have to send them home. Don't be a jerk about it, and don't humiliate anyone trying to do a good job. But make it clear that this job is not something just anyone can do. We're not here to get our little novelty diploma, a pat on the back, and a "Good luck!" When people can't keep up—and you will always have a few of those—do them (and your brand) a favor and let them go home.

There is no organization in the world that is the best at what it does that doesn't follow this training philosophy: the Marines, the Brazilian national soccer team, the Alvin Ailey American Dance Theater. If you are going to put your brand health in the hands of these people, you have to be tough. Because if your people aren't good, your brand is not going to grow.

Later on Day 2, announce that you are going out into the real world. Everybody will record themselves as they spend one hour trying to share stories about the brand with people. At the end of the hour, you will all listen to the tapes and discuss what worked and what didn't. This is horrifying for people, and they will express fear. Some of them will conquer it. Others won't. Better to find out now than when they're actually in the field.

Training Day 3

This is the day to bring it all together. They know about word of mouth marketing now, and they know a lot about the brand. It's time to run drills.

For this, it's good to have someone who is good at improvisation. We rely a lot on comedy improv teachers for this. They can really take the training to the next level.

Some fun drills to throw at them: Do a role-play during which the person they're talking to suddenly asks them to hold onto their dog for "just a minute" while they run to get food. Give them three minutes to tell you about the brand in iambic pentameter. If they say, "iambic what?" don't repeat yourself. If they can't figure out what iambic pentameter is in three minutes or come up with a convincing fake, they fail. Try it again. Work them hard on this. They should all be showing improvement by now.

All this time you should be breaking them of bad habits. These will continue to pop up until you drill them out of your trainees. Don't let those slide.

Training Day 4

In the morning, let them relax. Do something interesting and fun.

In the afternoon, more learning. Share more stories about the brand, and ask them questions about it. Do some more role-playing. Also, today is zero-tolerance day for bad habits.

Training Day 5

Wrap it up and send everyone home with a smile.

Ultimately, this is about stressing the ambassador system to find the cracks, and then fixing them before the ambassadors go out into the field. The Marines make it hard to get out of boot camp because it's hard to be out there in the field. The same should be true of your training.

If the product is particularly technical, training should go on for up to another week. In those cases, we will send trainees to the brand itself to immerse them in the subject matter. We call it "going to Brand School." Even if the product requires a PhD to understand, your ambassadors must be able to explain it to a 10-year-old in 30 seconds while his mother is calling him in for dinner. That sort of mastery comes only from a lot of education and a lot of practice.

Giving Ongoing Support

Training is only half the battle. The other half is supporting people who make good decisions based on their training. Even if it feels scary, or it isn't the way you would have done it, or it makes the boss uncomfortable. Often you will get pressure from above to rein in or correct someone who is actually doing a fantastic job, only not in exactly the way the boss wants it done. It's your job to prevent that person from being crushed.

Remember, we are training strategic corporals here. Giving people room to maneuver means doing precisely that. You can't run out there every time they make a maneuver you don't agree with. You have to support your people.

Even if your guy isn't using all the preferred language, if he's telling good stories, if he's getting people interested, support him. Brand ambassadors don't have to say the same thing over and over again. That's the point of doing your outreach this way. You have to let the influencers talk in a way that is natural and organic for them. And for that to happen, you have to stand up for them.

Remember, in a world dominated by conversation, they are your brand's first point of contact with potential customers. Years of bad experiential marketing have brainwashed us into thinking that brand ambassadors should be peppy airheads we train in a single afternoon. If you want to send strategic corporals into the field, you need to be running a boot camp—not a pep rally.

CHAPTER 5

A Matter of Patience: Measuring Word of Mouth Marketing

Measuring word of mouth is difficult and expensive. Tracking the movements of private conversations, then tying them to sales, is a task worthy of the world's finest epidemiologists. It requires a team of mathematicians and computer scientists and experienced data analysts working full time. This is why no one in her right mind, unless she works for a $5 billon company, attempts to do it herself. And even that person will probably turn to the experts, who are the very folks I'll introduce you to in the Appendix. These two people represent the best in word of mouth marketing measurement. They can help you understand the process far better than I can.

But first, as a word of mouth practitioner, I will show you how measurement fits into the bigger picture. Though you will ultimately outsource much of this work, you will never resign yourself to being a casual bystander. You'll be an active participant in your measurement. So you need to know what to expect.

THE LONGEST YEAR

If you launch a solid word of mouth marketing campaign today and stay with it for one year, then a year from today you will be sitting in your boss's office celebrating your sales increases. And on that day, your boss will not be asking many tough questions about your marketing strategy.

Every day between now and then, however, might be a different story.

Measuring word of mouth requires patience. Unlike other forms of marketing, doing a little today will not increase your sales tomorrow. It probably won't increase your sales this quarter either. Or the next one. That can be very hard to stomach, particularly for people accustomed to seeing sales spike after running a spate of TV commercials or print ads. Word of mouth marketing works slowly. It has to go slowly if it's going to work at all.

But word of mouth is both measurable and trackable. The trick is knowing what to measure before you begin. Figure that out, and you will clearly see it working along the way.

Then, before you know it, you will be popping champagne corks with the boss. You just have to make it through the year.

Cultivating Patience

If you have a boss who is more than 30 years old—and thankfully, most of us do—she will have grown up at a time when broadcast could move markets almost immediately. In those days, you could put a commercial on the air and see a corresponding lift in sales.

Hopefully, that lift would be greater than the cost of the commercials, so you could go back and make more commercials.

That's not how word of mouth works. Word of mouth is slower, but it is more effective over time. It takes longer to have an impact, but it will continue to pay off long after people have forgotten your commercials.

Why is that? Word of mouth must move at an authentic pace, and you can't hurry authenticity. Just as you can't force a flower to bloom faster than it wants to, conversations between influencers and their friends must happen at their own pace. If you try to hurry or force them, you will find yourself changing your tone from sharing to selling. And nothing turns off an influencer like being sold to. By attempting to move the tempo up or just seeming more anxious, you will turn a shareable story into a sleazy sales pitch. For word of mouth marketing to work, it must work slowly.

Unfortunately, too many ad agency executives have used "it takes time" as an excuse for a failing ad strategy. Consequently, when CMOs hear that phrase, they get suspicious. And who can blame them? But "it takes time" is true when it comes to word of mouth marketing, and furthermore, it is both necessary and desired. The slow pace lends credibility to word of mouth. You are allowing the influencer to deliver the message at his own pace. He may not see the person he wants to tell about your product for three or four weeks after he learns about it. He is talking about your product only when it is socially appropriate. He is not pushing it on anyone. That makes it both authentic and slow moving.

Unless you have invented a cure for cancer or baldness, stories about your product will move at a seemingly glacial pace. You have to be patient and stick with the plan.

Deciding What to Measure

The ultimate measure by which we are all judged is sales. We already know that your sales will increase at a slower rate with word of mouth than with other forms of marketing. But it is unreasonable in today's business environment to expect a company to make a marketing investment, then sit back and wait 12 months to know if it's going to pay off.

Luckily, there are other things you can measure along the way to see if your word of mouth campaign is working. Depending on what your company sells, you can decide ahead of time what those markers will be, and you should plan ahead to measure them. These are your *key performance indicators* (or, for the uninitiated, KPIs).

KPIs are your canaries in the coal mine. They will show you that interest in your brand is growing and that conversation is driving potential new customers to check you out. The trick for you is to find the KPIs that signal eventual sales. And your KPIs need to be sensitive enough that you will see them move before sales do. A large, glommy KPI won't work. By "glommy," I mean a metric that requires too many inputs, like overall brand health. Your KPIs need to be far more sensitive than that. KPIs that represent some part of the conversation process are best.

Here are a few examples of common KPIs that work. Some will work better for you than others. Your company might have some that aren't listed here at all. The idea is to get a sense and come up with a plan that suits your brand.

Digital Traffic

Is your website suddenly getting more hits? Are people going deeper into it than they previously were? Are you getting traffic from parts of the country that previously didn't pay much attention to you? Are you getting more Facebook comments?

These are all great indicators that people are taking an interest in your brand. (Website hits are also easily measurable. Odds are your company is already following these stats pretty closely.) Maybe these new visitors aren't buying anything yet, but they are checking you out. Keeping an eye on your website stats can both let you know your plan is working and calm an antsy boss.

Sentiment

A few months after you begin your word of mouth work, you should see an uptick in positive sentiment about your brand. Of course, sentiment is not something every brand tracks all the time.

The decision to conduct a survey before you start your campaign, then to repeat it, say, once a quarter, can soothe a lot of nerves (and frankly, sow a lot of excitement internally).

Sales of Small Items

One of our clients is an NBA team, and one way they can tell their word of mouth is working is through sales of team merchandise on game day. It's one thing to attend a game, but buying a T-shirt or a cap is making a statement. It's saying you are a supporter of this group, that you are a member of this tribe.

Ultimately, NBA teams want to sell more season tickets. That's the final goal. But that's a $5,000 to $15,000 commitment per season (per ticket). You don't need such big purchases to know if you're word of mouth marketing is succeeding. You'll know you're on your way when retail sales jump 25 percent in a year. That's a good, reliable KPI.

Forum Comments

Pay attention to how frequently your brand is mentioned in Internet forums. It should be happening more and more as you get a few months into your campaign. This is a sign that momentum and buzz around your brand is building among the people whose opinions matter most.

Measuring Advocacy

When it comes down to it, what you are trying to measure with these KPIs is advocacy. Sales will be your ultimate metric, but it's advocacy—people who are passionate about your brand and therefore recommending it to others—that drives sales.

David Rabjohns, one of the measurement experts I interview in the Appendix, says that his years of research support this idea. "The two things we found that really correlated with sales and share were advocacy and recommendations," he said. Everything I've experienced in my career says he's right.

But how do you measure that? The fact is, only people who are passionate about your brand will advocate for it. So when you're looking to measure advocacy, go to where people are passionate about your brand. Stop and ask yourself, Where might these people gather, so that I can watch and interview them? Usually, there is a physical place and a virtual place.

If you're a soccer team or a company that manufactures soccer gear, that physical place would be a professional soccer match. Or better, the World Cup. The virtual place, as stated above, would be an Internet forum or chat room where people prove their worthiness by their knowledge of and the intensity of their devotion to the subject.

Whatever tool you use, detecting advocacy means answering two questions: Is conversation about your brand happening? What is being said? Several months into your word of mouth campaign, you should be finding that people are talking about your brand and saying positive things. Hopefully, they are perpetuating the very conversations you have been trying to initiate.

As for which specific measurement tool to use, it really is up to you. There are as many measurement tools on the market as there are grains of sand on the beach. You have to find the one that's right for your brand, company, and product—there are simply too many variables for me to make a blanket recommendation here. But this is not about what tool to use. Pick your tool. This is about knowing what to measure.

THE QUESTIONS

Now that we've glimpsed the future, let's go back to the beginning. When you tell your boss or your colleagues (or your wife or your husband, for that matter) that you want to devote some resources to word of mouth marketing, you will inevitably get some questions. A lot of those questions will revolve around measurement:

- What are you going to measure?

- Why is that important?

- How much does it cost to measure that?

- How will you know that word of mouth is affecting that?

- How will you know how much word of mouth is affecting that?

They have a point. The only truly accurate way to measure word of mouth marketing is to get yourself a journal and follow everyone who is talking about your brand and write down everything they say and whom they say it to. Then follow those people around, too, and mark down who ends up buying what.

The further you get from that ideal, the more math you have to do, the more assumptions you have to make, and the more expensive measurement becomes, in terms of both time and treasure.

But guess what? This mathematical method is the same way broadcast, print, and outdoor advertising is measured. You cannot possibly track every TV viewer or magazine reader in the country. Instead, Arbitron and Nielsen sample a small portion of the TV-viewing public and extrapolate from there. There is not a network executive or media buyer in America who thinks this is a perfectly accurate system. But they have enough faith in the math to use it as the basis for billion-dollar deals.

Will you ever be able to answer these questions with 100 percent certainty? Of course not. But neither can anybody working with any other channel. The trick is to hire the right people and provide the right data. Beyond that, you simply must have faith in the math.

As with all things, the more money you have to spend, the less guesswork you will have to do. In 2011, AT&T—a company that spends more than $20 billion a year on advertising—decided to find out once and for all which of its marketing tactics was doing the most to drive new sales. To measure its word of mouth efforts, the company hired Keller Fay, a premier word of mouth measurement firm cofounded by Ed Keller (my interview with him is in the Appendix). The resulting report, for which AT&T won an Advertising Research Foundation award, found that its word of mouth efforts were responsible for 10 percent of sales volume, second only to paid media, which was responsible for 30 percent.[1] (If you have the time and you truly want an understanding of how word of mouth marketing can help drive sales for a big corporation, I highly recommend reading this report.)

Unfortunately, most companies do not have the money to perform that kind of forensic marketing analysis. And even those that do often choose not to spend it on that. We have a client with about $500 million in annual revenue that wanted to know how much state-of-the-art data collection would cost. When we told the company's leaders that it would cost 15 percent of their total marketing spend, they decided instead to put that money toward running the entire program for an extra month and a half. Others have increased their spend by 20 percent just to get those numbers.

As with any other kind of ad results measurement, the amount of money you spend to track word of mouth marketing will directly affect how good your numbers are. It is a matter of means and corporate priorities. Either way, it is not a DIY project.

PRO TIP

Don't cheat!

It is very tempting for anyone trying to measure their nascent word of mouth efforts to simply go online and sample some social media chatter. We will discuss this further in Chapter 8, but one of the greatest myths about word of mouth marketing is that, in the twenty-first century, it all takes place online. This is simply not true.

(continues)

In my experience, the vast majority of word of mouth conversations still happen face-to-face. And more important, the face-to-face conversations are far more influential than the virtual ones.

"It turns out that the offline part of word of mouth is far bigger than the online piece, despite the growth of online," says Ed Keller, one of the foremost measurement experts. "And though that part is not as immediately obvious to a lot of people, it is critically important to measure."

Measuring online is cheaper and easier, which will be very seductive to the people controlling your company's purse strings. But taking the easy road will ultimately cost you money in bad decisions based on flawed information. Take online word of mouth measurements as indicative of the whole, and you could end up short-circuiting a burgeoning campaign.

Throughout this process, you will have to balance the tension between money spent and mathematically valid measurements. The people above you may want to take the cheap, easy route. But there is no cheap, easy way to do this. You have to balance that tension, which is hard, but it's also what makes the whole thing effective.

What People Are Really Asking About When They Ask About Measurement

I am not a psychologist. But I have been doing this long enough to know a thing or two about the mindset of marketing people. In the word of mouth world, when someone asks a lot of questions about measurement, he isn't just asking about measurement. He is asking one of three things:

- Is this really going to work?

- How fast is it going to work compared to what I'm used to?

- How do you know this is going to work better than what I'm used to?

When someone is asking these questions, it means he is still trying to decide where to put his resources. That's as it should be. It is this person's job to decide what to do with his company's time and money. These questions should be asked. And they should also be answered as best as they can be. But more important is to answer the questions he is really asking.

Word of mouth marketing can seem weird and scary. I get that. This is not how your boss did it, and it is not how your company has done it. This is, in a sense, something new. And in this hypercompetitive American market, where people are looking at your results quarter by quarter, new can be terrifying.

When People Object to Word of Mouth Marketing

No matter how determined you are to try word of mouth, someone in your company—probably the person asking the most questions about measurement—is going to tell you he doesn't want to do it. He would rather put the company resources behind the thing that the company's been doing for years—even though it is perfectly clear to everyone that that thing has long since stopped working. I see this all the time. People would rather do the thing that doesn't work anymore than the new thing that they are pretty sure will because nobody ever got fired for doing what everyone did in the past.

When this happens, don't be discouraged. Just keep hammering away and making your case. Eventually, everyone will be doing word of mouth marketing because the truth is, it's what we've always done. We've just figured out a way to do it on purpose.

CHAPTER 6

Big Data: The Stories Within the Numbers

A good word of mouth marketing campaign centers on a story that is interesting, relevant, and authentic. But how do you know what's relevant to your customers at any given moment? One answer is to conduct consumer research, then examine the data for signs of what currently interests the people you're targeting.

These days, that can be a tricky proposition. Not because it's difficult to acquire up-to-the-minute consumer data but because there's suddenly so darn much of it. Between social media, loyalty programs, retail tracking, and a dozen other sources of digitized feedback, most CMOs are now drowning in data. Many are struggling just to store it all, never mind make sense of it.

I'm no data scientist, but I know a thing or two about finding the story in a swirling ocean of raw statistics. Fizz once helped a major chip manufacturer spread the word about a breakthrough that could seriously improve the way its chip processed information. At first, this company had us trying to sell everybody on clock speed and other wonky engineering specs. But one of my employees, an avid gamer, saw something else as he was perusing the chip data: the improved chip would make it possible to play first-person shooter and racing games without stutter (a gaming term for the maddening delay in frames that sometimes occurs due to lack of computing power or a decent Internet connection).

At Fizz, we are always thinking about subcultures and what might be interesting, relevant, and authentic for them. You should be too. It doesn't take a marketing genius to see that a chip that didn't cause stutter would be, for lack of a better term, a game changer for the gamer subculture. So we decided to talk to the most hardcore gamers out there. We demonstrated the chip for them and shared the technical info behind the improvements. We told them about the manufacturing process, the math behind the processing, the physics of electrons jumping from one gate to another—far more information than they needed but not more than they could handle. These guys then went to their gamer friends and told them about playing *Halo*, for example, with zero stutter, which generated a lot of excitement within the community.

The chip wound up being incredibly successful largely because it was beautifully engineered. But we were able to help supercharge its adoption among a key group of players because we knew how to read the data. We knew what to look for. And it made all the difference.

When it comes to Big Data, it helps to know what you're looking for, to ask the right questions, and to spend some time getting to know your own numbers. I can't help you store your data, but I can help you find the stories hidden inside.

AN ANCIENT PROBLEM

As business buzzwords go, *Big Data* has now achieved a level of ubiquity not seen since *synergy* or *downsizing*. But while the problems associated with storing and analyzing petabytes of digital data may be unique to our time, there is nothing new about the struggle to make sense of too much information. Pharaohs, kings, city planners, and industry leaders have all struggled to make sense of too many figures and statistics. But even as the details and quantities change, the principles remain the same.

The trick to getting value out of your data is not in how you collect or store it but in how you slice and dice it. The goal is to come away with information you can act on and insights you can use to help you make decisions. It's not hard to figure out what is going on with your customers. What you really want to know is why.

The Cereal Company That Learned Surprising Things About Its Customers

Consider the example of a cereal company that wanted to know how its customers were reacting to the financial crisis of 2008. How did the recession change their buying and eating habits? While sorting through reams of data gleaned from a social media listening tool, the company noticed two things. One, despite having less money to spend, the brand's customers didn't want to compromise on the quality of the food they fed their families. Two, they were very concerned about the quality of their garage.

This second part struck the cereal people as odd. So they went back to the data, and a pattern emerged. Many of these customers were buying in bulk for the first time, and they were storing the excess cereal in their garages. Some of them were even banding together to buy in mass quantities not seen outside the wholesale grocery business that they could share among themselves—a process known as *breaking bulk*. So now their concerns about cereal had grown to include the quality of their garage. Was it providing enough protection from snow and rain? Would it keep out foraging critters? And they were talking about this on social media in the same conversations they were having about cereal.

This was a valuable insight the company could turn into action. Maybe it could offer a plastic storage bin with every four gallons of cereal. Or use a better glue to seal its boxes so critters would be less likely to smell it. The point is, from all this data the company had acquired, it managed to focus in on one tiny bit of information—conversations about garages—and extract a story that helped it make decisions and engage more meaningfully with its audience.

The Why Behind the What

Approached correctly, Big Data is a tool that helps you see the why behind the what. This is vital to word of mouth marketing because you are trying to have conversations with groups of people who already have a preferred way of communicating with one another. Whether it's NASCAR fans or parents who buy cereal, these people are part of a group, and that group has a way of spreading its own information. If you want to insert your story, your only hope is to give them something they will pass among themselves. This means that your story must be relevant to their interests. By examining the data, you can see not only what interests them but why. That allows you to tailor your message more finely than any marketer could have dreamed of even 10 years ago.

If you know the why, you can tweak your story in just the right way. You can change its emphasis. Or you can go back to product development and make informed changes. Knowing the why lets you get into the minds of your customers and see the world, and your product, the way they see it.

Fifty years ago, marketers who were good at their job had a good sense of what was going on with their customers. They had empathy and insight. This is still true. But today, Big Data is there to amplify and sharpen those instincts.

This is particularly important in a splintered, heterogeneous society like ours. Fifty years ago, there were three networks to watch, a handful of movies in theaters at any one time, and exponentially fewer brands of spaghetti sauce on the shelf. Today, empathy and insight aren't enough. You can't really act on a hunch that parents in a certain region are storing cereal in their garages because they've started buying in bulk, or that twentysomethings in Boston are starting to buy your beer because a local band mentions it in a song. How would you even know these things?

Instinct and empathy are great, but you need data—lots of it— to tell you that.

Unfortunately, Big Data doesn't surrender its secrets easily. You have to be willing to put in the work, and you have to know how to approach it. The key is to break it down and to ask the right questions.

BIG DATA IS LITTLE DATA

Making sense of large data sets is a bit like putting together one of those 4,000-piece Lego projects. Take, for example, the Lego Death Star (actual piece count: 3,803). When you first open the box and see all those packages with all those tiny pieces, it seems inconceivable that it will all somehow become a coherent whole. Still, you open all those packages, and you group all the pieces by size and color and start to consult the instructions. Slowly, you begin putting things together.

Then, it happens. You realize that this one part you've been working on is the prison block and that other section is the trash compactor, and this one here is where (spoiler alert) Darth Vader kills Obi Wan Kenobi. Once you recognize the patterns, you can make faster decisions. Before long, you barely even need the instructions. You can see where this is going.

Making sense of Big Data works the same way. You are looking for patterns. You want to find little subsets that tell a story. In this way, Big Data can be seen as nothing more than many sets of little data put together. Ultimately, that's all it is. And it's useful to look at it that way.

It also helps if you know what you're looking for. If you had never seen *Star Wars*, you would never be able to recognize the scenes as they emerge. But if you go into it with a sense of what you want to see, you will start to recognize patterns much faster.

This is where your marketer's instincts come into play. You separate the signal from the noise in Big Data by being as specific as you can about the signal you're searching for. While you obviously won't know exactly what you're looking for until you find it, you should know your customers well enough to ask informed questions.

But you also have to put some work into getting to know your own data—something that fewer and fewer marketers are doing these days. That is an unfortunate trend, and one you should resist.

A Little DIY Goes a Long Way

To get the most from your data, you will eventually hire a professional analyst. With data sets that now routinely take up terabytes of storage space, it has become routine to turn to third-party vendors to make sense of it. There's nothing wrong with that. But be careful of allowing yourself to become alienated from your own data.

Analyzing data is a lot like sending your kids to school. Sure, they'll learn a lot there. But that doesn't let you off the hook from teaching them at home too. Likewise, just because you're paying some fancy analytics firm to decipher your data doesn't give you a pass on looking at it yourself. No matter how good your analytics firm is, it doesn't know your business or your customers the way you do. Besides, how will you know what questions to ask the analyst if you're not conducting your own research on the front end?

So take the time to go through your own data. Sit with it for a couple of days, and don't expect to find answers right away. The idea is to experiment. Come up with hypotheses. Follow leads, even if they appear silly at first. I promise that if you pay close enough attention and you put in the time, you will see patterns that eventually make sense. Then ask yourself, Why is this happening? And ask your analytics vendor the same questions. You will get far more out of your data that way than if you simply outsource it.

And ultimately, you want to be paying your analytics firm not to decipher your data but to sort it, categorize it, and find similarities within it for you. Then it's your job to search for the stories contained within.

The Right Questions to Ask

Some questions cannot—or should not—be posed to Big Data. "What's next?" "What do my customers want?" Big, vague inquiries like that will only produce big, vague answers. And it's hard to do much with such big answers in word of mouth marketing.

Better to focus on a couple of things you already suspect are happening, and try to understand what is driving those trends. If you've spent the time going through your own data, and if you combine that with what your marketer's instincts already tell you,

you should be able to pose good, specific questions to your analytics team that will yield real, actionable insights.

The more specific the questions you're asking, the more useful the information that you pull from the data will be. And you need to ask your questions in a few different ways. Sometimes, a small change in wording can make all the difference. Try four or five iterations of the same question, and you'll see that you get different answers. That alone will tell you something about how your customers are communicating.

In the end, you do want answers to big questions like, "What's next for my customers?" But you get them by asking the small questions. The Death Star, big and scary though it may be, is still just a collection of little pieces. Small, targeted questions are how you move from data to information. And for word of mouth marketing, it's information we need, not data.

I know Big Data can seem scary. But remember, in the end, it's just a lot of little data grouped together. As word of mouth marketers, it's our job to find the stories inside the data. When you're looking to start conversations that are relevant to your customers, there is no such thing as too much information, particularly in a fractured culture like ours. Just remember to put in the time, be specific about what you're looking for, and keep searching for the why behind the what. Once you understand that, you can join the conversation rather than trying to initiate one of your own.

CHAPTER 7

Save Your Money: Word of Mouth Marketing and Small Businesses

I'd like to take a moment to talk privately to my readers who own a small business. As you near the end of this book, perhaps you find yourself thinking that your business could benefit from a little word of mouth marketing. That's fabulous. Perhaps you're even ready to go out and find an agency to help you.

That would be a mistake.

If your company grosses less than $2 million a year, you do not need to hire anyone—an agency, a consultant, an intern—to help you execute a perfectly effective word of mouth marketing campaign. All you need is time and ingenuity. An outgoing personality doesn't hurt either.

DO IT YOURSELF

All successful small business owners have one thing in common. At some point, it occurred to you that your community could use a kid-friendly barber, or a plumber who works evenings, or an electronics store with a more knowledgeable staff. Then one day, you decided you were the person for the job. If you're still in business today, and you are reading this book, that means that you were right.

It also means your business is probably a good reflection of your personality and work ethic. In my experience, small businesses do well when their owner is deeply, personally invested. The way you treat your customers, the way you compensate your employees, what products you choose to buy and sell, the lighting in your dressing rooms—these are all creative choices that reflect your personality. And up till now, your marketing choices have been too. So why be in a hurry to hand those over to a "professional"?

This is particularly true when it comes to word of mouth marketing. Nobody knows your business better than you do. You know better than anyone what makes it talkable, and nobody could be a more authentic, passionate advocate than you. If the goal is to get more people to talk about your brand, no one is more qualified than you to start the conversation. You just have to figure out how to do it.

All the tools you need to perform a perfectly effective, reasonably localized (that is, not national) word of mouth campaign are already within your reach. You don't need to worry about New York, Los Angeles, Dallas, or Miami, unless your business is located there, so don't waste your money on an agency that provides national reach. You've already got everything you need to get people in your community talking.

You just have to start the conversation.

Taking Stock

Let's play a game. Take a moment to think about all your current marketing efforts. And by "marketing," I mean anything you are doing to make the case, directly or indirectly, that people should spend more money with you. That includes obvious things like radio ads, windshield flyers, local team sponsorships, coupons, and that A-frame chalkboard you put out on the sidewalk each morning. But if you own a restaurant, it also means your ingredients and the liquor you serve. If you have people answer the phone in a particular way, that counts as marketing.

Here's a small example from our own work growing Fizz. Our hold music is an old REM song re-created using only sound effects from the Nintendo video game Super Mario Brothers. When you are in the "creating conversations" business and something as banal as your hold music creates conversations, then that's a marketing point. We are sampling to potential customers how the everyday can become talkable and, in our case, how conversations about small but relevant things can lead to a broader discussion about a company and its services. In short, we are demonstrating how WOMM works and how it could work for the caller, our potential client, without ever having to say, "Now let me tell you how this works."

Your first job is to separate all of your marketing efforts into two piles. In the first pile are things that people might talk about. Not just what someone will notice and maybe even act on, but what might actually spur a conversation between people. In the second pile goes everything else.

I am not going to tell you to throw out that second pile just yet. Instead, we are going to put it aside for now. We'll come back to it. Because the truth is, nearly everything you do in your business can be made talkable. The most banal bit of outreach—putting a flyer on a windshield, for example—can be transformed into something that sparks conversations.

But it's the first pile that can fuel your word of mouth campaign more immediately. The things you already do that make your brand worthy of conversations between your customers and their friends— real, face-to-face conversations—are the things that you need to be focusing on. Maybe people are already having conversations about those things. That's great. We're going to talk about how you can increase and focus the conversations already being had.

PRO TIP

Amassing referrals is not the same as word of mouth marketing.

When it comes to small businesses, I have found that people often confuse *word of mouth* with *referrals*. These are not the same things. In reality, referrals are the result of word of mouth, the acts of people who admire your company enough to recommend it to others. But first you must forge that community, and word of mouth is how you do it.

Done correctly, good word of mouth marketing means you will never have to ask for referrals. They will simply be given to you, like birthday gifts. And like birthday gifts, no one over 12 years old should be asking for one. It's undignified. Get your word of mouth going, and conversation will occur about you and your business. Remember, influencers don't need to be reminded to influence just like singers don't need to be reminded to sing and writers don't need to be reminded to write. In all three personality types, it's what they do.

Face-to-Face Time

For small businesses, word of mouth marketing is about creating opportunities for two things:

1. Face-to-face conversations between you and your customers

2. Face-to-face conversations between your customers and their friends

We've discussed the significance of face-to-face conversations. Even as our lives become increasingly digital, actual in-person conversations still account for the vast majority of conversations between people in the United States. "Only 7 percent of word of mouth is online," says Jonah Berger, associate professor of marketing at the Wharton School of Business at the University of Pennsylvania and author of *Contagious*, a great book about influence and marketing. "Most is offline or face-to-face."[1] Offline conversations tend to be far more positive and memorable too. Social media has a role to play in spreading the word about your small business, and we'll talk about that in a minute. But if you want to get people talking, you need to be talking directly to your customers.

You and your decisions are the lifeblood of your company. You don't have 75 warehouses across the country and the ability to deliver anything for sale anywhere in the world for free in the next 24 hours. What you have is you, your brand promise, and your commitment to fulfilling that brand promise every day. To get people talking, you need to put those things right in your customers' faces, literally.

You need to talk to them. And you need to give them their two-ounce samples.

This is where you have an advantage over the big guys. Why reduce yourself to a faceless tweet, for example, when you can be a flesh-and-blood person shaking hands with potential customers at a county festival or a soccer game? If you're a car mechanic, let them see your dirty fingernails. Or if you're a pediatrician, let them see how clean your fingers are. Own a clothing boutique? Let them check out your snazzy pants. Face-to-face provides context that can't be duplicated online.

Don't worry: I am not suggesting you get out and "press the flesh" like some kind of cheesy politician. I'm suggesting you be your own brand ambassador. Here's a story that should explain the difference.

The Welcome Wagon

Fizz worked with a national chain of fast-casual restaurants. Though the chain itself was a large corporation, the general manager of each individual restaurant was responsible for his restaurant's profit and loss. So in that sense, each general manager was a small business owner. Unfortunately, because of all that responsibility, many of them were too busy to spend any real time with their own customers outside the four walls of their store.

We worked with one manager in particular who was responsible for a number of stores across the Midwest, some in small towns where there weren't a lot of restaurant options. Because of that, his restaurants had become more than places to eat. They were places for neighbors to gather and share news, for local sports teams to show off photos and trophies, for local clubs to hold meetings, and for students to celebrate after games or concerts. That was a huge strength, and it made these restaurants very talkable.

But not much talking was going on, largely because this manager was too busy managing to engage with the people in his community. So we advised him to get out of the kitchen and go meet people. Be neighborly. One specific bit of advice we gave him: If you see a family moving into a new house, go knock on the door and offer them a free meal. Just introduce yourself, hand over your business card, and say, "Welcome to the neighborhood. Come in anytime this week and have dinner on me."

Is it weird to walk up to a stranger's house and introduce yourself? Absolutely. For about 10 seconds. But once you've explained who you are and you've offered a free meal, that awkwardness is quickly replaced by warmth and neighborly gratitude. This is old-school Welcome Wagon stuff we're talking about. Only the most jaded person would find it irritating.

More important, the gesture was talkable. The second that front door was closed, the husband would turn to his wife and say, "Honey, guess what. The manager of that restaurant just stopped by to offer us a free meal. How nice is that?" And when that couple met their new neighbors, they would mention the outgoing restaurant manager who showed up at their front door. And so on and so on.

Once these people went to the restaurant, they would see that the manager was fulfilling on his brand promise, that this was a friendly neighborhood place where they could get to know their neighbors. The manager showed up to welcome them to the community, and what do you know? It turned out his restaurant could help them do just that.

In one year, that client tripled its growth rate. Not off that sole tactic, of course, but using a slew of like-minded approaches. The key was for the general manager—the small business owner, in this case—to get some word of mouth going by engaging with the community face-to-face.

Social media was not going to solve this problem. Would it be nice to get a tweet from the manager at the local restaurant inviting you in for a free meal? Sure. Is it as talkable as that manager showing up at your front door to shake your hand? Not even close. Face-to-face contact is essential in word of mouth marketing. And as the owner of your company, your face is the best one for people to see.

So ask yourself, Where can I interact with my potential customers? And how can I get my proverbial two-ounce sample into their hands? Home visits are not appropriate for every business. But that only means you need to find another venue. If you own a health food store, offer to do individual nutritional analyses for a local high school team (never recommending specific products or regimens, of course, because that would be selling, not sharing your passion for nutrition). You know your own business, so it shouldn't be hard to figure out where your customers can be found. That's where you need to be. (And you don't need help to get there.)

Talkability

If this plan is going to work, your story has to be talkable. Remember, that means it is interesting, authentic, and relevant to your audience. Two out of three won't work. That's why you have to perform the Brunch Test.

I've suggested that you subject your brand's story to the Brunch Test in a real-world situation. Not just in your mind, but with actual people who can give you honest feedback. The truth is, doing this is more important for small business owners than anyone else. As a business owner myself, I know that you often have more time than you do money (not that you necessarily have much of either). So carve out a little time to practice your story with family members, friends, and any employees who may be comfortable enough to tell you when you're wrong. Find other skeptical people. Share with them what you plan to share with your community, and see if their eyes light up. Only then do you have something truly talkable.

And remember, there is nothing neighborly about interrupting people. Hence the cardinal anti-rule of word of mouth marketing: never interrupt, never intercept. It can be tricky to follow sometimes, I admit. Plenty of people would consider a stranger knocking on their front door an interruption. That's why you don't do it at dinnertime or if you're offering anything less than a free meal (no knocking on doors with a coupon for a half-price muffler inspection, please). That's another reason to seek out people waiting in lines; hardly anyone minds being given something to do while they're waiting. And if you're engaging people at the gym, please don't do it while they're mid-squat. Best to set up and let them come to you. If they're interested, they will.

PRO TIP

Beware of the "Table Trap" at festivals and fairs.

Street fairs, block parties, and community festivals are great places to meet your neighbors. But be wary of the "Table Trap." If you take a table or a booth at these fairs so that you end up sitting behind a de facto barrier covered in brochures and sign-up sheets, you are not getting the most out of the events. You are literally boxing yourself in.

(continues)

Don't wall yourself off from the people you're trying to meet with a piece of furniture. It's nothing but a barrier to conversation. If you must have a table, opt for a round one. It's much harder to hide behind.

Making the Banal Talkable

Now let's go back to that second pile of marketing efforts. You know, the one with all the stuff that wasn't likely to spark any conversations. The coupons, the windshield flyers, the too-loud music that plays unrelentingly on your website. With a little imagination, there's no reason you can't keep doing these things. But you need to make them talkable.

There is a parking problem in downtown Decatur, Georgia, where the Fizz office is located. The area is populated by dozens of little stores and restaurants, which makes it perfect for an afternoon of shopping and snacking. But it gets crowded, particularly during the holidays, so some people stay away for fear of getting a parking ticket. A few years ago, the Decatur Downtown Development Authority came up with a great solution.

The association decided to buy all the time on all the meters in the neighborhood in the days leading up to Christmas. Then, when someone didn't pay for his meter, the police would place a flyer on his windshield that looked like a ticket (Figure 7.1).

This took some doing. The association had to convince the mayor and the chief of police to go along with it. And it cost a little bit of money. But that effort turned a rude, boring tactic—windshield flyers—into a fun, talkable event. The shoppers got a smile out

Figure 7.1 **Decatur "Traffic Ticket"**

of it, and the local media jumped all over it. That's proof of talk-ability right there. Now the association does it every year.

You can turn literally any marketing tactic into something talkable. You just have to be a little creative. Take some risks. Break out of the small business marketing mold.

If you can't find a way to make something in that second pile talkable, chuck it. It's probably not worth your time.

"But I'm Shy"

Not everyone is good at interacting with strangers. For some people, it's downright horrifying. I get that. But face-to-face interactions don't have to be conversations. Sometimes, actions can speak as loudly as words.

When I was growing up, there was an Ace Hardware store in my neighborhood that was owned by a man named Mr. Humphrey. Everyone called the store "Mr. Humphrey's." If you asked people in town "Where is Ace Hardware?" they probably wouldn't have known what you were talking about. It was simply, "Mr. Humphrey's." The man was a neighborhood legend.

Mr. Humphrey was not a talkative guy. You would never find him glad-handing potential customers at a block party, much less knocking on your door with an offer for a free drill bit. But if something in your home broke and you had no idea how to fix it, all you had to do was ask Mr. Humphrey. He would explain what you needed to do, then sell you everything you needed to do the job— and nothing you didn't.

When my grandfather was diagnosed with bone cancer, it fell upon my father to install handrails throughout his house so he wouldn't fall and hurt himself. For some reason, the hospital first discharged my grandfather at 6 p.m. on a Sunday, long after Mr. Humphrey's had closed for the day, leaving my father in a bind.

Luckily, Mr. Humphrey always kept an "in case of emergency" number posted on the door to his shop. My father called, and Mr. Humphrey came right away. Unfortunately, my father hadn't had time to take any measurements from my grandfather's house, so he didn't know exactly what he needed.

"Take whatever you want," Mr. Humphrey said. "What you don't use, bring back. I'll charge you for what you keep."

That story—just one of many great ones about Mr. Humphrey—quickly made its way around the neighborhood.

The point is, you don't have to be Bill Clinton or Mark Twain to get people talking about you. Yes, it would be ideal to get out there and start the conversations yourself. But you can run your business in such a way that it becomes talkable without your ever leaving the shop.

You don't even have to be nice. In my current neighborhood, there is a bagel store known as the "Angry Bagel." This is not its real name, of course. It's just a really good bagel shop with a staff that is known for being ornery, to the point that it's become a point of conversation among the locals. I have no proof of this, and they certainly wouldn't tell me if I asked, but I'm pretty sure the folks at Angry Bagel have intentionally stayed grumpy over the years because they know it's become part of their identity. And people love them for it. Because it's talkable, that grumpiness has led to customer to friend conversation.

If going out into the community and talking to people about your business is truly a problem for you, then what you need to do is figure out what is important about your business, what makes it talkable, and create opportunities for people to talk about it.

Employees

For better or worse, your employees are talking about your business. Does that make them natural assets in a word of mouth campaign?

Yes and no. Even employees who love your business aren't necessarily great for the job. As with any brand ambassadors, the key is to find natural influencers. If you have employees who fit the mold—they like new things because they're new, like to share stories with friends, and are intrinsically motivated—then by all means, use them. If they truly are influencers, they will jump at the chance to get out there and share stories about your business with the neighborhood. They might even be better at it than you are.

Just as important, never forget that your employees are talking about your company no matter what. They are members of the community too. Whether or not you like it, they are acting as brand ambassadors when they leave at the end of the day. No boss should make it her priority to be liked by all her employees all the time. But you should be careful not to send your employees out there with stories that contradict the ones you're trying to share.

Think of this as one more reason to be sure your stories are authentic. If it turned out that, behind the scenes, Mr. Humphrey was a tyrant or that the Angry Bagel folks were actually a bunch of pussycats, the story would be shattered, and the talk would turn ugly. Always share an authentic story, and you'll never have to worry about the truth coming out.

Digital Tools

The more you talk to people about your business, the more people are going to talk to you about the digital platforms your business "must" be on. These people are not necessarily wrong. If a potential customer goes looking for your company on Facebook, it would be a shame if she found nothing. Or worse, she found a similarly named competitor. Indeed, all sorts of social media tools are useful to small business owners for one reason or another.

But these days, only two social media platforms truly matter for word of mouth marketing.

Yelp and TripAdvisor

Unlike most social media tools, these two review sites represent a link in the word of mouth chain. Why? Because people use them to confirm or contest what they have heard from others about your business. Their reviews will never sway people as much as face-to-face recommendations. But they do hold the power to discredit the stories you've worked so hard to put out into the community.

At the moment, these two are the most important review sites. Of course, if you're reading this book 10, even 5, years after I've written it, there's a very good chance these sites won't be the big players in the review space anymore. They might not even exist. But no matter—the principles I'm laying out here apply to all review sites.

Here's how these sites work in relation to word of mouth: After a potential customer hears about your business from friends enough times, particularly if it's a restaurant or retail shop, he will check out some Yelp reviews to corroborate what he's heard. The same is doubly true for anyone going on vacation who is considering a visit to your restaurant, hotel, theater, or store. Vacation time is precious, after all. So it is best to use TripAdvisor to confirm what your friends said before committing time to a destination.

According to a 2013 survey from Angelsmith, a San Francisco website development and marketing agency, 20 percent of people search for additional information about a restaurant they've heard about from a friend before deciding whether to go there. In that same survey, 23 percent of people said that sites like Yelp and TripAdvisor held the most influence over where they decided to eat, second only to recommendations from family or friends (49 percent).[2]

Luckily, it is not a single good or bad review on these sites that will sway anyone's opinion. Consumers today, particularly those who seek out online reviews, are sophisticated enough to know that even the best restaurants will have an off night, or simply fall victim to Internet trolls. (Likewise, they know that your glowing five-star review probably came from either your publicist or your mother.)

We've never conducted a formal study on this, but our extensive anecdotal evidence suggests that the average Yelp reader looks at 8 to 12 reviews before deciding whether to patronize a business. What people are looking for is an overall sense of customer satisfaction before they dive in. So your goal is not to have a five-star rating on these sites, or even a slew of perfect reviews. What you want is critical mass—enough happy customers reviewing your business to neutralize any negative commenters.

Don't be afraid to ask your customers to review your business on either of these sites. As always, don't interrupt and don't intercept. But find a way to politely suggest they share their opinions online. Something along the lines of "We'd love to see your review on Yelp" is invitational, and therefore it is a perfectly polite, acceptable thing to say to a customer.

Do not ask customers to leave you a "good" review. And please, do not offer a discount for one. Doing so violates the terms of service of nearly every review site, and it is also a bit shady and obvious: nobody trusts a Yelp page filled with nothing but five-star reviews. Just ask your customers to share their experience.

If you're not comfortable saying that in person, get it made into an ink stamp at your local printing shop and print it on customer checks. Feel free to use any method of communication you like. As long as it's not intrusive to your customers' experience, then it's a good thing. Sometimes, simply putting the Yelp or TripAdvisor sticker on your front door is enough to encourage the site's heavy users to leave a review.

Engaging the Trolls

Playing in this social media space means tolerating the occasional negative review. Maybe it's deserved. Or maybe the reviewer was in a bad mood that day, or there was simply a misunderstanding. That's when you need to decide, will you respond?

In my opinion, responding to negative online reviews is a job only for the finest writers. Have you brought people to tears with your thank you cards? Did your love letters convince your wife to marry you? If so, go ahead and engage—politely and respectfully.

If you're anything less than a world-class writer, I would shy away from responding to negative reviews. Again, most Yelp users know a troll when they see one. Every business attracts some negative reviews. Best to absorb it and move on.

Facebook

Facebook and similar social networking sites are great for making cat videos go viral. Word of mouth marketing not so much. Again, Yelp and TripAdvisor are important to word of mouth because they are centered on user reviews of companies. The fact that someone *can* mention your company on Facebook doesn't make it a word of mouth tool.

To be sure, a local business should have a presence on Facebook, or whatever the popular social network is at the time you're reading this, simply because customers might search for your company there, and it would be a shame if they didn't find it. But in my experience, trying to stoke word of mouth on Facebook is almost never worth the effort.

Facebook echoes organic conversation. But first you have to make that happen.

YOUR COMMUNITY: EMBRACE YOUR PEOPLE

Mr. Humphrey never took a vacation. Everyone in town knew that. He was too busy tending to his store and all our hardware needs. So when it came time for him to retire, the town decided to pay him back. The neighborhood raised $9,000 to buy him and his wife plane tickets to travel around the world.

And when the big corporate bagel place moved into the same strip mall, fans of Angry Bagel went out of their way to stay loyal. Who did that company think it was, trying to replace our beloved bagel curmudgeons? People avoided the new place, and they gave as much business as they could to Angry Bagel. Which store do you think is still in business today?

If you engage authentically with the people in your region long enough and you fulfill on your brand promise every day, you will do more than sell more stuff to more people more often. Because you are having all these face-to-face interactions, and because you have become a subject of conversation in the neighborhood, you will enjoy something that very few large national companies get to experience: you will create a sense of community around your brand.

Once you are there, you will have a pool of people you can call on to help you in ways that will have a positive impact on sales. Remember, 10 percent of the people in any community have that influencer personality. Once these people are fans of your brand, they will go out of their way to tell others about you and to advocate for your business. You can't force that to happen, but you can inspire it with years of dedicated, authentic face-to-face interactions.

One of my favorite examples of this principle at work is Tito's Handmade Vodka. The company got its start when Tito Beveridge (real name), a geologist in Austin, Texas, who made his living in the mortgage business, started getting recognized around town for the flavored vodkas he made for friends. In the mid-1990s, Beveridge decided he wanted to go into the vodka business full-time, but he was rebuffed by bar owners. "The last thing I need is another bottle of off-brand vodka gathering dust on my shelf," they said to him.

So Beveridge set about making a better vodka, despite having no real idea how to do it. To test his recipes, he invited locals over for frequent tastings. As you can imagine, this engendered a lot of warm feelings and loyalty, even when the vodka wasn't so great.

Once his recipe was perfected, Beveridge called on these friends to help him get his vodka into bars. Anytime they were out drinking or having dinner, he told them, they should ask to speak to the beverage manager. "Why don't you carry Tito's?" they would ask. "We love Tito's!" Once a bar decided to stock it, members of the community would tell one another, and the bar would soon have to order more.

The strategy worked. In 2012, Tito's sold 850,000 cases and pulled in $85 million in revenue.[3] Yet in 2014, Fifth Generation, the first name that Beveridge gave his company in 1997, still employed fewer than 18 people.[4]

By constantly interacting face-to-face with his audience and giving them a sense of ownership over his product (and yes, getting them a little drunk), Beveridge forged a tight-knit community around his brand that grew alongside the brand.

In the age of digital media, the idea has taken hold, thanks to too many unqualified experts, that you can create this kind of community simply by tending to your Facebook page. Fizz's experience demonstrates the opposite. Once you have built your community through word of mouth and by delivering on your brand promise, a Facebook page is a great place to organize and interact with the resulting community. But you can't put the cart before the horse. Expecting a community of loyal customers to emerge from your Facebook page is like expecting to have a baby because you bought a crib. You've got to put in the work, and you've got to stay the course.

Word of mouth marketing is not an all-day thing, but it is an everyday thing. What are you doing today to create more conversations about your company tomorrow? What are you going to do next month? If you are always asking yourself this question and you are always working on an answer, you will find that once it starts to work, you will experience a geometric expansion of sales. Over time, the amount of money you put into these efforts will not increase, but the benefits you reap from them will.

This is where word of mouth differs from nearly all other forms of marketing. For a business, coupons offer a diminishing return—over time, customers won't shop at your store without one. If one billboard works today, you need to buy eight next year. But engaging face-to-face with your customers and potential customers every day—sharing an authentic, interesting, and relevant story that they can share with others and getting those two-ounce samples in their hands—reaps greater benefits the longer you keep at it.

Stay the course, and before too long, your small business will pass that $2 million a year threshold. When that happens, let's you and I get together.

CHAPTER 8

Myths, Lies, and Misconceptions

If you've come this far, you probably have a good bit of interest in word of mouth marketing. Soon, you may start talking to your boss, your board, or your colleagues about it. If that's the case, you should be prepared to confront the many myths and misconceptions that surround it.

It may be statements like "Oh, that costs too much" or "There's technology that does that for you already," or it may be a question like "Isn't that just social media?" All of these people come from a place of wanting the best for your company. In the many years that I've been doing this, I've heard every single one of them. By now, I've gotten pretty good at responding. Maybe I can help you do it too.

Some of the myths you will hear stem from simple misunderstandings. Word of mouth marketing is relatively new, after all, and the concept can seem strange to traditional marketers. Then there are the urban legends born of active imaginations and little knowledge.

None of these questions are unsophisticated or stupid. As with any other specialized practice, word of mouth marketing can be hard to grasp at first. Take the time to educate the person doing the asking. You never know. He or she just might one day influence the way someone else thinks about word of mouth marketing.

Myth: It doesn't matter where you launch your word of mouth campaign. When it comes to sharing stories, all U.S. cities are created equal.

You could launch a word of mouth campaign about your handbag in Upper Darby, Pennsylvania. You could seek out technology influencers in Flagstaff, Arizona. But that would be doing it the hard way.

Much like the weather, conversation in America follows some predictable and largely immutable patterns. Conversations about new fashion trends don't start in Billings, Montana, then knock around the Midwest for a few years until they find their way to Manhattan. Conversations have a natural flow, and any good word of mouth campaign is going to piggyback on that flow. Resisting it is futile and expensive.

There are certain cities in America—six to be exact—that we consider *leadership cities*. Then there are six *fast-follower cities*. These 12 make up the majority of the word of mouth engine in the United States (Figure 8.1). What these cities are talking about today determines what the other cities will be doing (and buying) tomorrow. If you want to spread your story as efficiently as possible, you need to start with six of these cities. Once you've captured them, you are on your way to capturing the country.

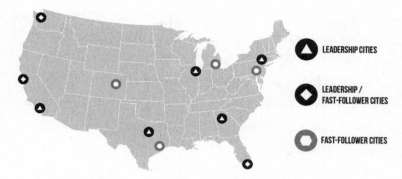

Figure 8.1 **Map of Leadership and Fast-Follower Cities**

The leadership cities are these.

Cities 1 and 2. New York and Los Angeles

Nearly all conversations about trends, products, ideas, films, books, or anything else you can think of in the United States seem to start in one of these two cities. This is for reasons of geographic density, but also tradition. New York and LA have rich cultural histories in the arts, fashion, media, and ideas. They are also centers of immigration.

Taken together, these factors foster a culture that values identifying things early and sharing them with others. Each city has its particular focus, of course. But in any given area, they are mere milliseconds behind one another, conversationally speaking.

City 3. Dallas

Yes, Dallas. Why? Unlike New York and LA, Dallas is a large, vibrant city built and centered almost exclusively on commerce and industry. Set in the middle of a desert, far away from any natural port or immigration hub, Dallas owes its very existence to private enterprise. Just try telling the history of Dallas without talking about Neiman Marcus, cattle, or the East Texas Oil Field. It would be like telling the history of Vegas without mentioning casinos.

Since its inception, Dallas has had a strong tradition of talking about things you can buy. It's always, "Hey, what's the new thing?" Combine that with the expectation that Everything Is Bigger in Texas, and you have the recipe for a great word of mouth town. All in all, Dallas is about half a second behind New York and LA.

Cities 4 and 5. Chicago and Atlanta

Both these cities serve as magnets for people in the surrounding states who want to do things a little bit differently or just to break out of their small towns. You want to be a musician, a chef, or a writer? Is your lifestyle simply a bit alternative? Maybe you just want to be different from your parents and grandparents.

If the answer to any of these is yes, and you were born in the American Southeast or the Midwest, odds are good you will end up living in Chicago or Atlanta. This fuels a natural obsession with what's new, with being slightly ahead of the place you came from. Chicago and Atlanta are about six months behind New York and LA.

City 6. Take Your Pick

The sixth city you target for your word of mouth campaign will depend on your product. Your choices are Seattle, San Francisco, or Miami.

San Francisco

If your thing is food, wine, chocolate, beer, or pretty much anything else you can eat or drink, San Francisco is your city. The City by the Bay has long been on the edge of all things culinary, and it is always looking for the new, new thing in that arena.

Today, when people hear "San Francisco," they think "technology." Until recently, San Francisco treated tech the way upperclass British people treat money: they have it; they just don't want to talk about it. That has changed. As the startup scene has moved north from Palo Alto, San Francisco has become increasingly tech centric. Today, everyone either works at a startup or knows someone who does. The conversation in the city has changed accordingly. So if you can get people in San Francisco talking about your startup, you're in good shape to get the rest of the country talking about it too.

Seattle

Seattle is ideal for "immediately useful technology." Rather than focusing on technologies that enable you to do something you couldn't do before, Seattleites love technologies that make something you're already doing easier. It's iterative rather than revolutionary.

Think about it: Microsoft Word is a better word processor. Burton Snowboards offer a better way of skiing. Grunge is metal without sunshine or hairspray. Boeing has been making airplanes better for 50 years. In Seattle, you have a very strong culture based on the next iteration of everyday things. If you have a technology that is useful to everyday life, you want to have a presence in Seattle.

Miami

Miami is sometimes called the "northernmost city in Latin America," and with good reason. The vibe of Miami is about celebration, fun, partying, bright colors, music, and nightlife. Tell someone that a new kind of strappy sandal is the hottest thing in Miami nightclubs, and a week later it will be selling out of stores in a dozen other cities. Any word of mouth campaign having to do with music, clothing, or the beach belongs in Miami.

Whichever two cities you don't pick from those three will be added to your list of fast-follower cities. The other four fast-follower cities are Denver, Philadelphia, Houston, and what we call "New Detroit."

Yes, Detroit. You probably haven't heard much good news about the Motor City lately. But at the moment, scores of young, hard-working people who are short on money but big on ideas— let's call them artists—are flocking there, beckoned by cheap real estate and the chance to build something new. It's Austin in the 1980s; it might even be Orange County in the 1930s. These people don't have a lot of money, but they have friends in places like the Williamsburg section of Brooklyn, Silver Lake in LA, the cool parts of Philadelphia—all of whom are eager to hear their stories. When my son is in college, all the cool stuff will be coming out of Detroit. So don't count out Detroit as a place to spread a little word of mouth. There are more cool people there than you think.

Sure, you can do word of mouth marketing in Indiana. Or Boston. Or Charleston, South Carolina. But if you want to go national as quickly as possible, the 12 cities listed, approached in this order and following these criteria, will spread your story faster and more efficiently, so you can get on with the business of selling more stuff.

PRO TIP

Identify an anchor city.

If your focus is regional, use one of the leadership or fast-follower cities as your anchor, and then focus on any surrounding cities that feed into your hub.

Myth: Word of mouth marketing is inexpensive.

It's not. In the beginning, word of mouth marketing will cost the equivalent of broadcast. But over time, if done right, word of mouth marketing can be substantially less expensive than broadcast.

As you know, the real cost in broadcast is not in making the ad (though that is expensive). The real cost of broadcast comes in renting someone else's network. If you want to spread your message, you have to pay money to take up space or time on someone else's system, whether that's a network of TV stations, people, or cell towers. Do as much broadcast advertising as you want—the cost of renting those networks will never go down. In fact, it will more than likely go up. The concept is known as *media inflation*. "Hey, you're making a half a billion dollars on this thing you're advertising? Well, now it's going to cost you $400 million to rent my network."

This is one reason I sometimes refer to broadcast as the "heroin of business." The first time you do it, you get this big bump in sales—a bump that exceeds what you invested. That's a big thrill. But over time, the more you try to re-create that bump, the harder it gets. The increase in sales is rarely as dramatic as it was that first time. And further harshing your buzz is the fact that the media guys keep jacking up their rates on you. After a while, you realize you're just chasing the dragon—a destructive and expensive habit.

For word of mouth marketing, the main price of admission to the network of influencers is the quality of your story and your ability to fulfill against it, day in and day out. If you're offering a shareable brand promise, and your company consistently delivers on that promise, then people will be talking about you.

But word of mouth marketing is not viral videos or flash mobs either. It is not something you do once for $2,000 and then walk away from it. In the beginning, it requires a real investment.

In today's dollars, a good word of mouth marketing program will cost $450,000 per market, per year. There are only 12 markets in the United States that you need to be in, but the minimum number of states you should be in is three, and you need to commit to the program for at least 24 months.

If you want to do it yourself, you can save about 30 percent.

Bear in mind, these numbers reflect both the amount of cash that you'll spend out in the field and the monetary value of the time your staff will spend on the campaign. But that's all there is. It won't cost more than this.

Nonetheless, these numbers sometimes surprise some people. They think that because it's new and nontraditional, word of mouth is going to cost something on a par with a handful of sponsored tweets. Sorry. Word of mouth marketing is like sex. If you don't go all in, it's not going to work. And it's going to get messy.

The good news is that there is also no such thing as an $80 million word of mouth marketing campaign. Because once you get those 12 cities we discussed, everybody else will follow. There is almost no limit to the amount of broadcast you can buy. And if you come to rely on broadcast, you may soon find yourself trying to buy as much as you possibly can in a futile attempt to re-create that first high. But in word of mouth marketing, a national campaign to make you the biggest thing in the world in just two years should cost no more than $8 million per year.

And the year after that, it will cost less. If you continue to fulfill on your brand promise, then people will continue talking about your brand. They will keep sharing your story as long as you stay awesome.

In the end, the amount of money you have to spend annually on your word of mouth program will decrease by about 10 percent of the rate that your sales are increasing. If you're growing 50 percent a year, you can probably drop your total marketing spend for word of mouth by about 5 percent every year.

Word of mouth marketing may be more expensive than people think. But in the long run, it is far less expensive than broadcast. And, of course, much more effective.

Myth: Bloggers hold more influence than ordinary people.

Most research firms have long since given up trying to track how many blogs are launched every year, much less how many people are actually reading them. Even Technorati, whose annual *State of the Blogosphere* report had been among the most-cited sources of blogging statistics since 2004, apparently stopped conducting it after 2011. But given the way things were going, it is now safe to say that reader stats for your average blog are sadder than click-through rates for banner ads. In other words, most blogs today probably have an average readership of less than a single person. That is assuming the blog hasn't been abandoned by its proprietor, like the vast majority of blogs launched in the past decade (95 percent, according to the 2009 Technorati report).

Yet many marketers remain obsessed with kissing up to bloggers as if they hold some special power. If you are selling something a mother might find useful, someone is going to insist you send all manner of swag and invitations to a dozen or more mommy bloggers.

This is a waste of time and swag.

Can bloggers be influential? Absolutely. But simply being a blogger does not make a person more influential than anyone else. The tools facilitating person-to-person communication have been so democratized these days that anyone can have a massive reach, with or without a blog.

A blog is just another tool, and a blogger is just another person who may or may not have an influencer personality. In the context of word of mouth, focusing more on someone simply because he has a more public forum in which to express his views doesn't necessarily make sense. Plus, it can easily backfire.

Because marketers forget that bloggers are ordinary citizens, not journalists, they tend to try too hard when courting them, often by sending them all manner of free stuff in a very sales-pitchy way. And what do we know about true influencers? They don't react well to being bought. Now you've gone and irritated a potential influencer with a public forum. Maybe this person will have no sway over others, but maybe he will. In my experience, it's just not worth the risk.

If you want to have a conversation with a blogger, then have a real conversation with her. Maybe you'll be interested in the same things, and then she'll share what you have to say with her audience. But bear in mind, when it comes to audiences, the only difference between a blogger and an influencer is that nobody is measuring how many people the influencer is talking to. Don't assume a blogger's audience is bigger just because she has stats.

Myth: Celebrities are influential.

When it comes to identifying influencers, the rules for celebrities are the same as for anyone else. Are they passionate about the product or service? Do they use it and talk about it in their everyday life? Do they love to share stories with others about it? If yes, then you may be looking at an influencer. But being a celebrity does not automatically make someone influential, especially not in our atomized, hyperspecialized culture.

Think about Oprah Winfrey. Oprah enjoys a good book, and she has set up a massive network to share her passion with others. She's also a great storyteller. So yes, you would have to call her an influencer. But remember, it's not the size of the megaphone that matters.

What makes Oprah special is that she has an influencer personality that people can feel through the television, and that is very rare. But her power to move markets is not unique. There are all kinds of people across the country who can say, "Oh my gosh, you should totally buy this thing for your son or your husband for Christmas; he will love it," and have huge numbers of people listen to them.

When it comes to word of mouth, people aren't influential because they're celebrities. They are influential because they are passionate about your thing and like telling people stories.

One of my music clients is really, really into video games. So much so that his audience knows it. And there was one game in particular—an online game about music—that he liked so much and felt such an affinity with that he decided it should have a character based on him.

He contacted the company's leaders and proposed that they make such a character, and he would voice it. Naturally, they loved the idea—not because he was superfamous but because a lot of people knew he was into their game. Hence his involvement meant something. It was an actual endorsement, in the true meaning of the word. And naturally, the video game company assumed this musician would tell everyone about his involvement with the game and recommend they play it. Which he did.

We have other clients who are much more famous than this guy. But nobody knows or thinks about them as video game fans. Had one of them gone to this company and asked to become a character, and had he promised to share it with his millions of Twitter followers, it would have been essentially useless. Why should a hard-core gamer care what some nongamer rock star thinks about a video game? It's not about the celebrity. It's about the passion.

Whatever the category, I promise that I can name a dozen influencers who can help you move more product and help you get more stories out across the whole country faster than any celebrity. Why? Because people who are really passionate about those categories and involved in the communities surrounding them already know and listen to these influencers. And they do their best to stay informed about those categories. In turn, the people who follow them know they will not waste their time with useless, inauthentic information.

You cannot buy that kind of celebrity. You have to earn it, and then you have to continue to earn it by constantly sharing new information.

Once you start seeing the world in terms of word of mouth, you realize that everyone is a celebrity to someone. And those kinds of celebrities are the ones who move product.

PRO TIP

Be careful with celebrity endorsements.

In late 2012, Ana Gasteyer, a former cast member of *Saturday Night Live*, began tweeting incessantly and hilariously about her obsession with Weight Watchers:

> Hey @WeightWatchers: I binged on Children's Gummy Vites. Can it be my cheat day?

> Hey @WeightWatchers: How many #activitypoints for wrestling a cat into a carrier? About 23 mins/very sweaty. Pls note w/without swearing. Thx.

Eventually, some smart executive at Weight Watchers contacted Gasteyer with an endorsement offer. Naturally she accepted, and the ensuing commercial spawned an avalanche of positive coverage for the brand. What a great example of empowering a celebrity who is also an authentic influencer— someone who self-identified, who came to the brand, as real influencers always do.

Compare that with Weight Watchers' decision to sign re-tired NBA star Charles Barkley as its new celebrity spokesperson,

(continues)

which took place at about the same time. The company un-veiled Barkley to the press with all the fanfare of the Rose Bowl Parade. Was this former basketball player and infamous rabble-rouser a natural influencer on the topic of diet plans? You tell me: Just weeks after his first commercial aired, Barkley was caught on camera calling his endorsement a "scam."

Here's the thing to remember about celebrities: They are people, not platforms. Treat them accordingly.

Myth: All adopters are influencers, and vice versa.

To the untrained eye, it is easy to mistake a smart, well-informed hobbyist for an influencer. But the difference is actually quite stark. Take my Uncle Bill. Uncle Bill is an extremely smart guy. When I was a kid, he loved to play Trivial Pursuit with me—until he got bored, which he inevitably would. When that happened, Uncle Bill would start trying to win, and 10 minutes later it would be over. In other words, I had a shot only as long as Uncle Bill wasn't trying.

But for all his intelligence and education, I don't think Uncle Bill once in his entire life has said to anybody, "Hey, I saw this thing the other day, and it made me think of you. Let me tell you all about it." This is true for huge portions of the population. They are smart, they are up-to-date, they are extraordinarily well read. But they don't feel compelled to share any of this information with other people.

This is why marketers often mistake early adopters for influ-encers. Just because you're among the first thousand people to use a computer program or a phone and you love it, doesn't mean you feel the need to tell anyone else about it. Many so-called early adopters are happy to keep information to themselves.

Thus it rarely makes sense to target your message to the first 500 people on line to buy the new iPhone, for example. They may be early adopters, but that doesn't mean they are influencing anybody. It doesn't mean they are sharing stories about their purchases. Early adopters and influencers may overlap, but they are not the same thing.

Steve Jobs knew the difference way back in 1983. That's the year that Steve Jobs hired Guy Kawasaki as his "chief evangelist" (a pretty progressive title for 1983). At the time, Apple already had good, innovative products that had attracted legions of dedicated followers. These people were very early adopters. But Jobs was ahead of his time, and he realized that these followers weren't necessarily spreading the word. They were just talking among themselves. What he really needed was someone with the technical knowledge of an early adopter who also got great joy from just sharing stories with people. Anyone who now follows Guy Kawasaki on Twitter, where he has more than a million followers, knows that this guy is a natural when it comes to sharing stories. Jobs put Kawasaki in charge of spreading the word, and because he had a good product and a great story, word spread pretty well.

So yes, influencers tend to be well informed, bright, and early to the trends. But that's not enough to make someone an influencer. It's the ones who are compelled to share their knowledge with others in an attempt to build bonds. That is the first and most defining characteristic of any true influencer.

Myth: Paying an influencer damages his credibility and robs your campaign of authenticity.

I know a guy who's been a working musician for 30 years, despite never being able to make a living from it. He has his day job, and then at night, he gigs around town with a couple of different bands. He gets paid for these gigs. But, according to him, he's never in his life been paid to play music.

"You don't get paid to perform," he told me. "You get paid to load the van. Performing, that I do for free."

Likewise, people who think that paying an influencer robs him of his credibility don't really understand what motivates an influencer. They also don't grasp what it is you're actually paying him for.

You are paying an influencer not to talk about your brand but to file reports, stand around in the rain, get out of bed when he's not feeling well, and participate in a weekly phone call. All the grunt work that comes with word of mouth marketing. And yes, you are paying him to talk about your brand more often than he normally would. Or, more accurately, more often than he normally *could* because he would have to be doing something else to make his money.

Influencers love to share stories about things they are passionate about. Paying them to do that doesn't compromise their credibility. Instead, it enables and empowers them to spend more time doing something they really want to be doing.

If you're paying someone to say nice things about something he doesn't particularly like, then yes, neither your campaign nor your "influencer" will have much credibility. But true influencers won't take money to endorse a product they don't care for, particularly if it's part of a category they're passionate about.

As long as an influencer never tries to conceal the fact that he's being paid, there is no reason that the people he talks to should ever consider it a stain on his credibility. If you love a certain band, and you find out that someone you know is now being paid *by the band* to talk to you about it, why would you be anything but jealous? I wish someone would pay me to talk about REM all day. And if ever I come across a fortysomething husband and father who has that gig, I am going to beg him to sign me up. All my other REM-loving friends will be jealous, and none of them will suddenly think they can't trust what I have to say about the band. Quite the opposite: They will start calling me for the latest info because they'll know I am "with the band." To a true fan, what could be cooler than that?

Myth: Word of mouth marketing? You mean social media.

There is no doubt that social media platforms such as Facebook and Twitter have changed how word of mouth is spread. And any good word of mouth campaign is going to take advantage of those tools.

But social media and word of mouth marketing are no more exclusive partners than Match.com and romance. The vast majority of human interaction still takes place in person, and the stuff that happens face-to-face is far more impactful than anything taking place online.

I know it may not seem that way after your third consecutive hour scrolling through Facebook. But according to a 2012 study from Ed Keller and his company, Keller Fay, 75 percent of conversations in the United States—and even more in other countries—

still take place face-to-face, while less than 10 percent take place online. That's not even close.

The rise of social media has led to a reduction in e-mail conversations, according to Keller Fay, but it has had no discernible effect on in-person communication. What's more, "face-to-face conversations tend to be more positive and more likely to be perceived as credible, in comparison with online," Ed and his partner, Brad Fay, wrote in a 2012 *USA Today* column.[1] "What people talk about online differs dramatically from offline. The former tends to be driven by what is perceived as 'cool,' while the latter tends to be about sharing real life experiences."

If your word of mouth campaign is focusing solely on social media, you are missing 90 percent of the conversations people are having every day, and an even higher percentage of the ones that matter. Online, the signal-to-noise ratio is practically deafening. Offline, people are still listening to one another. No word of mouth campaign today should be foolish enough to ignore social media. But even more foolish is mistaking it for the whole shebang.

Myth: There are now algorithms and technologies that can identify and rank influencers better and more efficiently than people can.

This may be the biggest whopper of them all. There are several companies out there that claim to have solved the influencer mystery. Using an algorithm of their own invention, they can assign people an influencer "score" based on their online behavior, they say. The idea is that you can decide whom to target your marketing messages to based on these scores because you'll know who is most likely to spread your message effectively.

Whether you are a company whose name rhymes with *trout*, or some close copy, the reality is that tech is not even close to producing a formula that can rank and sort influencers with the efficiency and accuracy of a human being. At the moment, the world's greatest artificial intelligence (AI) can mimic the behavior of a being about as complex as a dragonfly. Maybe in a few years, AI will be able to mimic a frog and small reptiles. But we are a long way off from technology that can understand, let alone mimic, the human mind. And that's what it takes to figure out who is influential and who is not. (I won't even get into the absurdity of trying to determine such a thing based solely on a person's social media presence.)

Think about the technology that's used to serve advertising online. If you've spent the past five years saving your pennies for a trip to Fiji, you will start seeing banner ads for trips to exotic locations the day after you finally buy your ticket online. Yet never in your life have you been less likely to buy a plane ticket. This is about the best a computer can do when trying to understand human behavior.

Need further proof? Just check out the influencer scores of some people you know. For example, if you're reading this book, you probably know who Bob Garfield is. If you don't, he is one of the all-time most respected advertising journalists and commentators. He has been a columnist for *USA Today*, the *Washington Post* magazine, and *Ad Age*. Today, he is probably best known as the cohost of NPR's *On the Media*. Any way you slice it, Bob Garfield is influential.

Yet Bob Garfield and I usually have the same influencer score. With all due respect to me, that's just wrong. But there it is for all the world to see: Ted Wright and Bob Garfield, blood brothers in influence. Sorry, but anyone who creates a software program that says Garfield and I are equally influential has either not nailed how to measure influence or doesn't understand the term.

When it comes to analyzing a person's influence or knowing whether he's an influencer at all, there is not yet any substitute for the human brain, particularly one that has spent years working with influencers. Are there computer programs out there that can help? Sure. But by no means can they do the job. Not yet, at least.

CHAPTER 9

Talking to Your Boss About Word of Mouth Marketing

CASE STUDY: FIZZ, INC.

Nobody on Earth woke up this morning excited to read some company's mission statement. How could anyone care about something so banal? Yet we at Fizz recently managed to turn our mission statement into something very talkable. It cost us no money, and it required very little effort. What it did require was a little bit of risk taking on our part.

The time had come last year for us to update our website. It was looking, shall we say, a bit 1990s. What we wanted was a site that would better reflect the Fizz ethos. We pride ourselves on putting a priority on what we think is right and not letting a client's internal politics get in the way of profitable growth. In a nutshell, we follow the rules that make the most sense to us. We're comfortable with that, and anyone who is going to work with us should be too. So we wanted our website to reflect that.

For example, if you visit our Team page, you won't find headshots of our employees. Instead, each person is represented by his or her favorite album. We've got everything from *Rage Against the*

Machine to Lil Wayne to John Denver with the Muppets. It's a fun, slightly irreverent way to give people a taste of who we are, and people who see it always tell us how much they like it.

But the real conversation starter is our mission statement. If you look at the top of our home page, you will notice something unusual. Like most companies, we have a link to our mission statement, except ours is labeled "NSFW."

If you don't already know, NSFW stands for "not safe for work." It's Internet shorthand for "Don't click on this if your boss is nearby" because it's either pornographic or it contains foul language.

It is not something you typically see near a company's mission statement.

But the Fizz mission statement is, and always has been, NSFW—which is half the reason it had never previously been on our website. (The other half being that I thought mission statements were boring and nobody ever reads them anyway.) It's there now because we asked ourselves what a corporate website could look like in 2014. What would happen if you put your mission statement right at the top of your page—a very 1990s thing to do—and labeled it "NSFW"?

It turns out you can create some pretty good word of mouth.

Our mission statement is simple: "We don't fuck around." That's the whole thing. But we figured that required some explanation. Here's what you find if you click on the Mission Statement [NSFW] page on our home page:

> "We don't fuck around"—that's Fizz's mission statement.
> If you are ever lucky enough to work here, you get a t-shirt
> with that printed on the back. It's our short way of saying
> that we do killer work, we are a great place to work, only

smart and interesting people work here, and we deliver huge ROI to our clients.

Here's the background to our mission statement, in our CEO's own words: "When I was 10, my Dad gave up his 9–5 job, bought a company, and over the next 8 years grew the annual revenue from 8M to 984M. When I was 17, he was diagnosed with brain cancer. A year and 37 days later, he was dead. At his funeral it occurred to me that he was always happy because he loved what he was doing in his personal, as well as professional, life. Right there I decided that I would be happy always. That has meant being very self-directed and honest with myself about what brings me joy. Having a killer team, living on the cutting edge, being rebellious, being right—these are the things that bring me joy, thus Fizz was created and has grown along the path it has taken. If this strikes you as the kind of people you want to work with, then please call us. We'd like to talk to you."

It turns out that if you put an NSFW link on your home page, everyone will click it. Then, two things happen.

First, once people finish reading it, they will keep clicking around on your website. We have always tracked the traffic on our site, and we know that after we added that mission statement, it greatly increased the amount of time people spent there. We can see that people take the time to read the statement, and then they want to know more about us. They go to our People page (where they see the album art), they go to the page where we describe our approach, and they even check to see if we have any job openings. That mission statement gets them interested in who we are, and they take the time to try to learn more.

The second thing that happens is everyone asks us about it. And I mean everyone. Recently, I was in a pitch meeting with a major insurance company, when the big boss, a very straight-laced woman, looked right at me and said, "What does NSFW mean?" I thought I was in trouble, but once I explained, she let out a huge laugh and regaled the whole room with the story of how she first encountered our mission statement, after which she shared it with her entire team. (It was a fabulous way to start a pitch meeting.) I have gotten calls from people just to say they loved the mission statement and wanted to know more about us.

I assume there is a third reaction too. The statement probably turns people off to Fizz. Some folks read that statement and decide they don't want to do business with us. That is both fine and totally expected. We knew when we put that link up that we'd be alienating people who don't appreciate our word choices.

But the fact is, if you are offended by that statement, you probably wouldn't be a good client for us anyway. If your small company is going to have an authentic, relevant story, it is naturally going to resonate with some people more than others. We don't believe we've missed out on any valuable clients because of that mission statement because those people wouldn't have stuck around very long anyway.

The point is, if you're going to get people talking about your small company, you've got to think about what makes it talkable, then create situations from which conversations can ensue. It won't take much money, and you don't have to hire anyone. You just have to take a risk.

Everybody has a boss. I don't care if you're the CEO, the chairman of the board, or the president of the United States. We all have someone we answer to, whether it's your spouse or Congress. And if you're going to make big changes, you're going to have to get buy-in from the boss.

Investing your company's money in word of mouth marketing, particularly after decades of trusting broadcast, is a big change. So let me help you make your case to the boss, whoever that may be.

A piece of advice before we proceed: Don't look at this as a chore or some nagging inconvenience. Having a boss makes you better. You know who didn't have a boss? Muammar Qaddafi. Saddam Hussein. George Lucas when he made *The Phantom Menace*. Checks and balances force us to make smarter, more responsible decisions. If you take this exercise seriously, you will emerge better prepared to lead your company into the world of word of mouth marketing.

NO MORE SQUIRRELS

Your boss has already seen enough squirrels, so the last thing you want to do is bring him one more.

I'm not talking about bushy-tailed rodents here, but about the litany of "latest and greatest" marketing ideas—those glittery, shiny objects that have waltzed through his door over the past decade. Viral videos! Sponsored tweets! User-generated content! Around the office, we refer to these as "squirrels" for their ability to lure perfectly intelligent people into fruitless pursuits, like dogs in the park. If you're the CMO, someone at some point—be it a board member, a coworker, or the boss—is going to come into your office and ask, "What are we doing about *X*?" Of course, *X* is the latest, greatest thing this person's daughter or nephew is into. So you end up committing resources to X, which inevitably disappears up a tree.

You don't want your boss to think word of mouth marketing is just another squirrel. This is why you should explain why you want to do it before you explain what it is. You need her to understand that this is not a shiny, new object. It's a new way of thinking made necessary by a shifting environment.

THE WHY BEFORE THE WHAT

There are two ways you are going to show your boss why your company needs to change its approach to marketing. The first is to provide a list of third-party data that shows how the mechanics of influence, particularly among your customers, have shifted away from broadcast and toward word of mouth.

Data

We live in a golden age of research, which is a huge advantage when you have reality on your side. Before you approach your boss, you should compile a list of relevant data that shows how your customers no longer take their cues on what to buy from broadcast but instead from friends and family, particularly through face-to-face interaction.

There are many great resources for such data. Among them are these:

1. Advertising Research Foundation: ARF.org

2. Word of Mouth Marketing Association (WOMMA): WOMMA.org

3. Harvard Business School (HBS): HBS.edu

4. Any of the following books: *The Anatomy of Buzz: How to Create Word-of-Mouth Marketing* by Emanuel Rosen; *Contagious: Why Things Catch On* by Jonah Berger; *The Chaos Scenario* by Bob Garfield; and *The Face-to-Face Book: Why Real Relationships Rule in a Digital Marketplace* by Ed Keller and Brad Fay

You want to compile 10 to 20 bullet points that show your boss how your particular customers have changed their habits. Your goal is to shift his perspective so he can appreciate the enormity of peer-to-peer influence in today's marketplace. The data you present should depend largely on your product and target demographic. Curate the stats to make the best possible case to your boss.

Game Time

Another way to help your boss understand the need for change is by using the following thought experiments. These are games designed to make the situation personal by showing her that she has shifted her habits as much as anyone.

The Billboard Game

Back in Chapter 1, I presented a version of this game as a fun trick to play with friends at parties. But here is where it truly comes in handy. Assuming your boss drives to work, ask her to tell you about the billboards she sees during her commute. The average commuter sees at least 10 to 20, depending on where she lives. Can your boss name half of them? Three-quarters of them? It's doubtful she can name all of them. When she is unable to, remind her that companies are paying for those eyesores on the assumption that she will not only see them but act on them.

If you really want to have fun, ask her how many products she has bought, or television shows she has decided to watch, or restaurants she had decided to try because she saw one of those billboards.

If the billboards aren't working on her, she should realize, they probably aren't working on anyone else either.

The Friends Versus TV Game

For this second game, you get to play a body language expert. Ask your boss to think about all the commercials she sees on television. Then ask her when the last time was she bought a product because it was advertised on one of those commercials. Odds are, as she thinks about it, she will make noticeable eye movements, looking this way or that as if the answer is hidden somewhere in the room. In our experience, this suggests someone is accessing long-term memory. In other words, she really has to think back a ways to find an answer.

Now ask her when was the last time she bought or chose something because a friend recommended it. Most likely, she won't move her eyes much at all, meaning she doesn't have to think very far back. Go ahead and alert her to her facial movements. She may be a little embarrassed, but you will look smart. And your point will be made.

Of course, you can play this game without alluding to her facial cues because her answers will make the point itself. Few people these days can remember the last time they bought something because of a commercial. We are all constantly following the recommendations of others. Again, life is easier when reality is on your side.

THE WHAT

Now that you've explained the why behind word of mouth marketing, it's time to tell your boss the what. Hopefully, at this point, she'll be eager to hear it.

What follows is an outline for your presentation. Follow this, and you should be able to make a cogent, persuasive argument that word of mouth marketing is more powerful than your challenges.

The Theme

As you know by now, at the heart of every word of mouth campaign is a story. You need to give influencers a story about your brand or product that is interesting, relevant, and authentic that they can share with others. To start your presentation, you are going to tell your boss the story of your brand or product.

What is it that is going to get people talking? And don't just tell her the story. Tell her why people will share it with one another. What makes it interesting, authentic, and relevant to your potential customers? Explain to her how the result ultimately will be more people recommending to their friends that they buy what you're selling.

Give her a brief primer on influencer personalities too. Explain that 10 percent of the population influences the buying, TV watching, and even voting habits of the other 90 percent. Explain how these people are naturally inclined to share stories with each other because that's how they form bonds with people. Explain why the influencers who are naturally passionate about your category will find your story interesting and pass it on to others.

The Tag Line Trap

Unfortunately, a lot of people who were raised in a broadcast mindset will listen to an interesting, authentic, and relevant story about their own brand and think, "Great, but how do we shave that down to three to five words?" This is a by-product of a lifetime searching for tag lines or slogans. What she wants to hear is the witty, memorable quip that will make the case for your brand, not the nuanced, multifaceted story you've just presented.

To counteract this, you will need to explain two things: (1) themes versus stories and (2) time differences.

Themes Versus Stories

The original *Star Wars* movie (*Star Wars IV: A New Hope*, for those of you keeping track) contained a lot of different stories. But all those stories centered on a single theme: the triumph of good over evil.

There was the story of the naive farm boy who craved adventure; another one about a political rebellion against a violent, fascist regime; one about religion versus technology; one about a hard-luck smuggler who, it turned out, cared more about friends than money.

But even if you didn't follow any of those story lines—which, as children, most of us couldn't hope to—you were still completely invested in that movie. Why? Because you always knew who the good guys were, who the bad guys were, and what they needed to do at any given moment to win. The stories were complex and overlapping, but the theme of good versus evil was always present and palpable.

Throughout this book, we've been talking about the story behind your brand. But for word of mouth marketing purposes, we could just as easily call it your "theme." The truth is, a good brand story is never monolithic. It has threads and subplots and nuances that people can decide to investigate more fully depending on their interests. Your brand story should be like *Star Wars IV: A New Hope*. It should have a theme, but within that theme should be many different threads that people can dive into.

Your story should not be like *Star Wars I: The Phantom Menace*, in which your enjoyment of the action sequences hinged largely on your ability to grasp the significance of an interplanetary trade embargo.

Influencers are better conduits for your brand story than print or TV ads because they tailor it to the individual. An influencer will give his drummer friend a different reason to check out the new Katy Perry album than he will his 10-year-old niece. Influencers use stories to forge bonds with people, so they are incentivized to make those stories personal. This is why your story needs to be like *A New Hope*. You need to explain to your boss that a certain amount of complexity here, as long as it doesn't obscure the overall theme, is a good thing. You want to give influencers enough story to work with so that they can tailor it to their audience.

Time Differences

Unlike a TV commercial, time is not compressed with influencers. They don't need to get all the information out in 30 seconds or less. They have as much time to talk as they want, provided they keep it interesting.

This is another reason you don't have to worry about creating a tagline. You don't have to hook people instantly. Let the story unfold naturally. It's one of the luxuries of word of mouth marketing, and it should be an incentive for your boss to buy into it, not a deterrent.

Activations

How aggressively you engage the public should be determined by the importance of what you're trying to sell. If you're offering something that the consumer would agree is central to his day-to-day life, you can be pretty direct.

Such a product warrants a more aggressive stance. But if you're approaching people about something they don't use every day or even think about very often, it's best to let them come to you. There are still other times when it's best to tell your story visually.

Activation Elements That Tell the Story Directly

There are times when it's acceptable, metaphorically speaking, to take the consumers by the lapels and say, "Do this!" You never want to hector, and you never want to interrupt. But if your product category is something your consumer already thinks about or uses every day, there is a slightly higher bar for what constitutes an interruption.

Of course, if you're going to be direct and you're not literally saving anyone's life, it helps to be playful, maybe even a bit over the top. The trick is to find a degree of humor appropriate to the product and situation.

Fizz has a client that offers home cable and Internet service using fiber optic technology, which delivers data far faster and more efficiently than cable. Because most people watch TV or use their computers at home every day, the product allowed for a more direct approach.

Still, this is essentially an entertainment product, so we wanted to be direct but fun. How could we make it OK to just walk up to people and tell them this product was good for them? We decided to play off the similarities between fiber optics and dietary fiber—namely, that both "move things along" faster. The central concept was that "everyone needs fiber."

We took our cues from the cereal wars of the 1980s, when brands competed to offer as much fiber as humanly possible. We broke down those campaigns and copied every element—tiny cereal boxes you handed to people as they got on the train in the morning, public service announcements (PSAs), health posters—all with text about fiber optics versus cable.

It was direct, but it was fun. Just don't lie to yourself about how important to a person's life your product really is. And yes, context matters. If you're talking to people about a comic book at a comic book convention, you can be much more direct than if you were talking to people about it in a hospital (an awful idea, for the record). It's important to strike the right chord.

Activation Elements That Tell the Story Indirectly

Most of the time, you are going to be telling your story indirectly. Though it pains us to admit it, as marketers, the stuff we are selling is rarely vital to a person's everyday existence. When that's the case, your best approach is to engage people passively. Let them come to you.

A perfect example is the Bissell sweeper program I mentioned earlier. Go where your potential customers are likely to gather—in this case, moms standing in line to see a mall Santa—and demonstrate your product where you can be seen but ignored if the consumers are just not interested. Those who want to learn more will take the initiative.

Is it possible to be too coy? Probably. But in my experience, this is not a problem most marketers have. Far harder is resisting the urge to be obnoxiously in-your-face. Always better to err on the side of coy.

Remember, for word of mouth marketing to work, you need to trust that people are intelligent. The reality is, there is no one on the planet more savvy to marketing messages than U.S. consumers. You don't have to spell it out for them. Throw the bait in the water, and the fish are perfectly capable of deciding for themselves if they want it.

Activation Elements That Tell the Story Visually

Regardless of how central your product is to someone's life, there are times and places when marketing messages are simply not appropriate. The last thing a surgeon attending a conference wants is one more pharmaceutical rep handing her a free pen. Or maybe it's just too dark, or too bright, or too hot. In these cases, it's best to tell your story visually.

That means creating an intriguing visual that will entice people to come to you and ask questions. Find a good spot that your target can't miss, and have brand ambassadors on hand to answer the inevitable questions. Don't be afraid to be bold. If the visual doesn't raise questions in the minds of people who see it, then it won't do its job.

It helps to have a visually interesting product. But it's not a requirement. Bottles of chocolate milk, for example, are not particularly eye-catching. But build a wall of them and place a bunch of pro athletes standing in front of it, and you will inevitably get questions. (See the Pro Tip "Try a Visual Campaign.") The trick is to juxtapose the product with the environment radically enough that people will be strongly compelled to investigate.

PRO TIP

Try a visual campaign.

In 2009, the dairy association came to us for help getting preteens and teenagers to drink more milk. On our side was recent research showing that chocolate milk was the best thing to drink following strenuous activity. It helped repair torn tissue, and it provided the energy needed to bounce back quickly.[1] This was a story worth talking about.

We asked ourselves, Who is best to influence the habits of middle school students? The answer was high school students. And how do you get high school students to drink chocolate milk following strenuous activity? High school coaches.

In order to engage high school coaches, we began showing up at football clinics. But these are tough places to grab a coach's attention. These guys were busy and already besieged by people hawking equipment, supplements, you name it. So instead of trying to address them directly, we would take over the longest, most well-trafficked hallway we could find, and we would fill it with ceiling-high, glass-door refrigerators packed with chocolate milk. Standing in front of the refrigerators were guys who looked like they had played in the NFL or Major League Baseball, because many of them had.

It was an arresting visual that told an intriguing story. Clearly, there was some connection between chocolate milk and athletic performance. Sure enough, about 1 out of every 10 coaches came up and started a conversation with our brand ambassadors. "What's with all the chocolate milk?" From there, the rest was easy. *(continues)*

After these coaches chatted with our ambassadors, we would watch them take some chocolate milk and sit down with other coaches. Inevitably, those other coaches would ask him to explain the chocolate milk. Thus word spread about the value of chocolate milk as a post-workout recovery drink.

By 2012, chocolate milk sales in the United States had increased 475 percent. ESPN, *Men's Health*, and the *Los Angeles Times* all picked up the story. And most telling to me, I received a call from a friend who happened to run a major grocery store chain. He wanted to know if I thought kids had figured out how to make drugs from chocolate milk. "No," I said. "Why do you ask?"

"Because I have video of herds of teenage boys and girls coming in to our stores and scraping all the chocolate milk off the shelves and into their carts," he said. High school and middle school athletes were buying all the chocolate milk they could get their hands on. Clearly, our campaign had worked.

In our experience, the average word of mouth marketing conversation lasts 32 seconds. You don't need to talk to people for long. You just need to find a way to start the conversation. Or, more accurately, let them start it.

Just know that there are a variety of ways to make that happen. Choosing the right path means knowing your brand and your activation environment. When talking to your boss, it's important to present the right kind of activation for the product and place. If you do, she will see that you're not just getting this from some word of mouth marketing playbook but that you have truly thought it out relative to your situation.

Questions

Before you give your presentation, take some time to anticipate the questions your boss and others in the room are likely to ask. I realize that this is covered in Presentations 101, but it's also one of those things that's hard to do and feels a bit goofy the first time. You'll be tempted to blow it off. Don't.

People are going to ask questions, and they will be legitimate questions. Remember, you are challenging, and possibly frightening, these people. What if they don't make their numbers? Why should they trust you? This is something very different you are asking them to do, and different is scary, particularly when your job is on the line. So take the time to think about each person who will be in that room, anticipate what questions those people might have, think about the answers, and write them down. Then do your best to memorize them. Nothing sinks a good presentation like a presenter who suddenly goes silent when faced with a couple of hard questions.

Unfortunately, the hardest question you will get is one you will not be able to answer—at least not to anyone's satisfaction. "If word of mouth marketing takes longer to get results than broadcast," someone will ask, "how am I going to make my numbers this quarter?"

The truth—and please don't throw this book out right now— is that they might not make their numbers this quarter. Or the one after that.

But if they take the alternative route, if they refuse to change their current approach to marketing, the time is coming when they will never make their numbers again. All the data shows that the time when you could throw a bunch of commercials on the air and get a bump in sales that exceeded the cost of the ads is long gone. If it weren't, Sears wouldn't be in the shape it is now, and American car companies would not have had the problems they have had for so many years.

You can risk your company's future by focusing on the next quarter, or you can secure it by thinking four, five quarters ahead. Yes, the first year of word of mouth marketing takes some fortitude. But it beats watching your company die a slow, painful death as it sinks money into a malfunctioning system.

I promise you, when your company sees this work, it will never go back to the old way again. And if you nail your presentation, you could be the hero who put it on the right track. So don't skip this step: Practice your answers beforehand.

Presentations

Always remember Guy Kawasaki's 10/20/30 rule: All presentations should consist of no more than 10 slides; they should last no more than 20 minutes; and the text on those slides should be rendered in 30-point font. If you can't fit what you have to say into those parameters, then whittle down what you are trying to say.

The idea here is not to lecture but to start a conversation. Your boss is not going to remember the slides. She won't even remember the specific statistics after a while. What she will remember is the conversation you started that day about how your company needed to change its approach. And she will remember who proposed the solution.

SUCCESSFUL SISYPHUS

Your goal is to sell more stuff to more people for more money. The truth is, there is no easy way to do that. For much of this book, I've contrasted word of mouth marketing to broadcast and other traditional forms of advertising. It's true that word of mouth is by far the smarter approach when people would rather take their cues from friends, family, even strangers on the Internet than commercials or billboards. So segmented is the United States these days that people with specialized interests—which is pretty much everyone—put their trust in the people they have access to who have the most experience in those areas, not mass media or advertising. But neither word of mouth marketing nor broadcast is easy.

Broadcast is like running on a treadmill. It seems easy at first because every time you take a step, the ground moves a bit beneath you. That serves as a little reward every time you lift your feet, and it keeps you going. The problem is, no matter how fast you run, you'll always finish right where you began. It takes a lot of effort, and you're never going to get anywhere.

Word of mouth marketing is like pushing a giant rock up a hill. At first, it seems impossible. Make one false step, and you can lose a lot of progress. Stop too long to take a breath, and you're in trouble. You've got to put in a little bit of effort every day, and some days that rock is going to roll backward. You're going to get frustrated, tired, and discouraged. You are going to feel like Sisyphus.

The difference is that you are actually getting somewhere.

One day—sooner than you think—you will get that rock to the top of the hill. This will be, quite literally, the tipping point, the moment your story catches on. Once you're there, you'll let go of the rock, and it will begin to roll on its own momentum. Before long, it will be speeding along, crashing through boulders and trees and discarded treadmills. Your sales will be growing 30, 40, 50 percent. And you'll just be watching the rock roll along, reaping the benefit of your hard work and the tough decisions you've made.

This is not pie-in-the-sky stuff. This is what we've done for clients, time and time again. You say this is scarier or riskier than the way you've always done it? We agree. Running on a treadmill is far easier then rolling a rock up a hill. But at the end of the day, no one is judging you on how safe your decisions are. They're judging you on results. You can point to the readout on the treadmill and say, "Look how many miles I've run!" But if you're standing in the same spot as when you started, you're not really impressing anyone.

If you took the time to read this book, you're not the kind of person who's happy just appearing to make the effort. You're not the satisfied-just-to-have-a-job person. So hopefully, you're not afraid of a little risk and hard work either. If you choose to put your trust in word of mouth marketing, it's not going to be all lollipops and roses in the beginning. You're going to spend a lot of time pushing that rock up the hill. But ultimately, this work will make the biggest difference in your business for the least amount of money. You will sell more stuff to more people for more money without breaking the bank. That's what everybody wants. And that's the best reason I can think of to try word of mouth marketing.

Be sure to tell your boss.

The Measurement Experts

David Rabjohns is the founder and CEO of MotiveQuest, an "on-line anthropology" company. If you need to track and decipher what is being said about your brand online and how it is affecting your sales, MotiveQuest is the company to call. Simply put, when it comes to measuring digital word of mouth, David is the man.

Ted: Why measure word of mouth?

David: When you live in a world where people bypass traditional marketing and turn to each other to decide what to buy, measuring word of mouth becomes the fundamental way to find out if you're making a good product, one that is serving people's needs. It's a measure of *remarkability*. Are you making a product that people can talk to each other about? In word of mouth, remarkability becomes a key performance indicator (KPI), so measuring for that becomes crucial.

Ted: How do you measure it?

David: We've struggled with this. I've been in business 10 years. For the first 3 years, we just had piles of data pouring in, and we really had no idea which data really mattered. We had buzz, we had sentiment, we had influencers. So I went over to Northwestern University and found myself a statistician. What we did was measure whether any of the things we were looking at correlated with sales and share. Interestingly we found buzz didn't correlate. Neither did things like blog audience size. The two things we found that really correlated with sales and share were advocacy and recommendations. And so the way we measure it is, we look at all the linguistic ways that people recommend something, from "I recommend" to "Check it out." We weight the different words because "I recommend" is more powerful than "Check it out." We create a forced-choice algorithm that separates out the net recommendation. Simply speaking, the best way to measure word of mouth marketing is to measure advocacy.

Ted: How do you define *advocacy*?

David: I think what you're trying to evaluate is, Where do I sit today? What's my situation? Are people talking about me or not? Is my product remarkable? Or should I fix it? And have I found a way to connect with people in a meaningful manner? I think you're looking to understand what's going on with your relationship with your customers. What do they care about, and do they care about you? For example, in the food and beverage category, only 5 percent of all conversations mention any brand at all. So if you're a pickle company, for example, you've got to work pretty hard to figure out what people care about that you can attach yourself to that might give people a reason to talk about your brand. Sauza tequila did this brilliantly. They bought Skinny Girl Margarita.

Nobody wants to really talk about tequila, but everybody wants to talk about skinniness, especially women, so that brand took off.

Ted: How do you go about hiring a vendor to measure word of mouth?

David: The first thing you're looking for is data quality. As with any kind of research, crap in is crap out. You've got to have good data. And different kinds of data work in different ways. Twitter needs separate analysis from forums or blogs. So the first thing is the quality of the data and the quality of the way the vendor analyzes the data.

The second is the linguistic strength of the vendor's analysts. How good are they? How comprehensive is their way of understanding the world of what people are talking about? For example, we did a study with Visa where one vendor told them they were the most talked-about brand in the 2008 Olympics, and the one most negatively talked about. We found that they were actually the twelfth most talked-about brand, and they were the most positively talked-about brand. The difference was the linguistic coding. The first vendor included all the complaints people were making about getting visas to get into China. So linguistic coding is crucial.

Then the third thing is some framework for making sense of the piles of data and enabling you to make decisions. There are an awful lot of dashboards that tell you what is going on with your brand online, but they don't tell you why. What you need is something that gives you some dimensions to look at your data within so you make smart decisions. Think the BCG Matrix but with word of mouth–specific categories. So what is the framework of thinking that can help you turn data into decisions, versus just having more data?

Ted: What should a good measurement campaign cost?

David: I'd say $10,000 to $20,000 a month. My CEO likes to say, "You can have it good, you can have it fast, you can have it cheap. Pick two."

Ted: What are the benefits of measuring word of mouth?

David: There are three major benefits I see. The first is finding new gaps in the market that you can expand into. Finding opportunities for growth and new revenue.

I think second is developing your tribe, figuring out who those people are who really love you already, and how to energize and activate them so you attract more people to the tribe, so you can therefore sell more stuff.

The third thing is maintaining ongoing engagement. I think that brands today are less about marketing to people than about building relationships with people. And I think if you don't know what's changing in your tribe, how they're talking differently about the things that matter to them on an ongoing basis, it's very hard to build a deep relationship with them. Really understanding what matters to your people on an ongoing basis matters because that drives sales.

Ted: What is the biggest rip-off in word of mouth measurement?

David: I think there's a lot of snake oil out there. I think there's an awful lot of beautiful charts and flashy software you can buy, and by the third month into the relationship, you realize that they're not helping you make meaningful decisions. Certainly in some departments, if you're in PR, for example, knowing what the crisis du jour is and reacting to it is important. But I had one client that was spending 75 percent of his time responding to negative comments. We did an analysis and showed him that 15 percent of all his customers were in that group of negative commenters, and that group was never going to change its mind no matter what he did. Meanwhile, he was leaving behind the 20 percent who loved his company and advocated for it. So I think data pouring in without perspective, without strategic advice—that's probably the biggest rip-off.

Ted: When it comes to measuring online word of mouth, a lot of people think they can do it themselves because they know how to search Twitter and use Google. What are the pitfalls to doing it yourself?

David: First thing is lack of perspective. People try to measure brand stuff by putting in keywords. Put in "Oreos" and see what comes back. But to understand the big picture, you need to look at things at a category level. And it's very hard to look at the category level because you need to get category data, and you need to have software that can read category data. You must also have the wherewithal to actually do the analysis—to break things down and segment things and understand them.

The second thing is lack of talent. If their car breaks down, most people will take it to the garage to get it fixed because they need someone who has had a lifetime of experience fixing cars. Likewise, analyzing huge amounts of data is incredibly complex and requires lots of experience. The hubris that you can do that yourself in a couple of days is kind of crazy.

The third thing is just objectivity. I think most people can't see their own brand for what it is. But people who are looking at lots of brands all the time can help you understand contextually how your brand stacks up versus the rest of the world.

Ted: How can a brand manager demonstrate to her boss in real time that word of mouth is working? If she can't, what's the minimum lag?

David: If you want, you can measure online word of mouth daily, hourly, by the second. And I think in some industries—if you're in financial services, for example—that might actually be appropriate. But most people can't react quickly enough. The market moves so dramatically that daily metrics are not even very useful. Maybe for customer service daily metrics matter because you're trying to jump ahead of customer service problems. But for anything strategic, anything that's about real marketing or brand building, I think you're better off stepping back and seeing the woods for the trees. You're better off not being bombarded with the daily stuff so you can see the patterns in the data. That's my experience. Most companies can't even react to the monthly data they are receiving.

Ted: What will be the big challenges for measuring word of mouth in the future?

David: Education. I think we're still at ground zero on word of mouth measurement. I think it's a bit like the first day somebody built a telescope and looked out at the universe: all he could see was one star. He really had no idea there was a whole universe out there to explore. I think we're kind of there with word of mouth measurement. People don't even understand how complicated it is—and at the same time, what enormous opportunities there are if they can just think about it the right way.

Ed Keller is cofounder and CEO of the Keller Fay Group, and he is one of the premier authorities on word of mouth measurement. He is coauthor of *The Influentials*, largely recognized as a seminal work on word of mouth marketing. In short, nobody knows face-to-face marketing better than Ed.

Ted: Why measure word of mouth?

Ed: People want to know two things. One, what's working and what's not? And two, if they're investing money, are they getting something out of it? The more you measure, the smarter you get. Whatever works this time, if you measure and understand what drives success, you can be more successful next time.

So if word of mouth wants to become an important part of the marketing mix, it needs to prove its value, and it needs to prove that it's worthy of time, attention, and investment. Thankfully, there are a growing number of people in many parts of the marketing discipline who realize the value and importance of word of mouth, and I think a good reason for that is because there has been more measurement.

Ted: How do you measure word of mouth?

Ed: Today when people think about word of mouth, a lot of them think about social media. So they're thinking about ways to measure tweets and likes on Facebook and so on. And the digital part of word of mouth is big, and it's growing. But there is a much bigger part of word of mouth, which is the part that's taking place offline. People talking at home, at work, people talking in bars and restaurants, churches and temples, and on the sidelines of soccer games. And it turns out that the offline part of word of mouth is far bigger than the online piece, despite the growth of online. And though that part is not as immediately obvious to a lot of people, it is critically important to measure.

Who people were talking to, what was being discussed, whether any media marketing was a part of the conversation. How credible is what you heard? How likely are you to purchase? These are all important things to measure.

Ted: What are the downsides to trying to do this yourself?

Ed: The analogy I would use is people who like to invest their own money without getting advice from a professional money manager. There are a lot of tools that enable people to monitor word of mouth on their own, and if you're good at analytics and you have the time to invest in really understanding what's happening, then I think some of those tools do a perfectly good job. But at the end of the day, people have other things to do, and so they don't spend as much time really mining the data to look for stories as often as they should.

The other potential pitfall is that there are always new tools and new techniques. The world of Big Data mining is getting better and better by the week. So doing it yourself may mean not taking full advantage of what's out there. People who are in the business of providing services in this area are better equipped to make sure that the analysis remains up to speed.

Ted: When it does come to hiring a third party to do your measurement for you, what are some good things to keep in mind? How do you evaluate a good vendor and decide whom to hire?

Ed: The thing to figure out is what kind of experience people have, and can they talk knowledgeably with you in a way that resonates with you? If you're hearing things that make sense to you, if someone's asking you the right questions about what you're trying to achieve, and then they come back with a proposal that is clear and understandable to you and fits your objectives, then that's probably a good fit.

You shouldn't feel intimidated by statistical or technical language. Someone should be able to explain the process and results to you clearly in a way that makes sense because at the end of the day, the research is only as good as you and your company's ability to interpret and understand it and implement it. So if it's not making sense to you, then you should probably spend some time looking for someone else.

Ted: What should a good measurement campaign cost?

Ed: I wish there was an easy way to answer that. It's like asking, "What's a good ad budget?" Excellent measurement can be done in the $20,000 to $40,000 range, but for a larger and more extensive program, it might cost as much as $100,000. At the end of the day, research is really driven by how many people you need to be getting information from over what period of time, how many brands are part of the mix, and so on.

Ted: In a multifaceted campaign, how do advertising and word of mouth marketing complement one another?

Ed: The goal of all media and marketing should be to spark conversation. Our research shows that in more than 50 percent of all word of mouth conversations, people are talking about an ad they saw or something they saw online or on a product package. That said, people are more skeptical of what they hear and see in advertising. So we really do think these two have to work hand in hand.

When people see an ad, often they'll pick up a certain message and then go have a conversation about it with somebody they know and trust. Similarly, if you've been given the opportunity to have firsthand experience with a brand, then the next time that you see an ad or read something on a website, what you see or hear ought to be consistent with your experience. When that happens, you have an opportunity to tell somebody, "Hey, I had a chance to try that product, and it is exactly the way it looks in that ad." And all of a sudden that ad has a lot of credibility, and that person in turn will tell somebody else.

A number of our clients these days are engaged in market mix modeling, and they're looking at all the different variables and trying to understand what impact each has in creating sales and new-customer acquisition. We strongly, strongly, strongly encourage that those market mix models should include word of mouth in them. When that happens, people end up discovering that word of mouth has a big impact directly, and all of a sudden it helps to illustrate to the CMO or CEO that word of mouth isn't something that's just nice to have. It is contributing in a very meaningful way. And when you can see exactly what the dollar value of your word of mouth is, it makes the company much more focused on what it can do to help that word of mouth.

Ted: How can a brand manager demonstrate to his or her boss in real time that word of mouth is working? If that's not an option, what is the minimum lag time?

Ed: If you've got a program whose real value is going to come over a time period of weeks or months—I've heard some companies say that the real impact of word of mouth advocacy might take as much as nine months—I would make sure that the client knows that, and then I would build in monthly or quarterly reports because there's nothing worse than having something that's reporting daily when nothing is happening. So you need to make sure that your speed of reporting is consistent with the expectation of when change has a reasonable chance of being measured.

Ted: What is the biggest fallacy in word of mouth measurement?

Ed: There is an idea out there that social media equals word of mouth. People say, "We have word of mouth covered because we've got a social listening system in place." Well, there is some excellent academic research that illustrates very clearly that people post things online for a set of reasons that are wholly different from why they have conversations offline. So it's a mistake to think that what you're measuring online is a mirror of what's being talked about offline because the minority of word of mouth is taking place through social media.

Ted: How do we know that influencers are real?

Ed: Well, we know they are real because a number of different people using a number of different research techniques have all come to similar conclusions. And that is that there are certain people who have a certain psychological makeup that gives them joy from sharing stories with others. They enjoy engaging in conversation with a wide variety of people. They like to get and give advice. They keep up with things that are new, and as a result, they get sought out for their advice.

Let me also say that some people criticize the concept of influencers by suggesting that some people think only influencers matter. "Oh, people say 1 in 10 Americans tell the other 9 everything they need to know, as if the other 9 have no impact at all." It's an invalid criticism. To the best of my knowledge, nobody who works in the influencer field has ever said that only influencers matter. What I think many of us who are in this area have said is that the evidence is clear that there are certain people who are more likely to be seeking out information. They're receptive to marketing messages. They have more conversations with other people, and their conversations have more credibility and more persuasive power. We call these people "influencers." If you are going to invest money, why wouldn't you want to invest money in that group, where you are more likely to have a greater bang for your buck?

Ted: Going forward, what are going to be the biggest opportunities for measuring word of mouth in the future?

Ed: A growing number of companies are coming to the conclusion that word of mouth can be managed and measured. A few years ago, there was an assumption that only brands that couldn't afford significant marketing budgets needed to be engaged in word of mouth. Now I think brands realize that word of mouth can help any brand. A while ago, people would say, "Look, I understand that word of mouth matters, but there is nothing I can do about it. It just happens, so I'm going to focus my attention on things that I can control." Some people still say that. Well, you can't control word of mouth, but you certainly can help to manage it by engaging in product development and in marketing activities that will help to increase positive word of mouth. And there's new research that's come out from the likes of the Boston Consulting Group that provides clear evidence that if brands can get more positive advocacy, it definitely drives top-line growth. And the gap in top-line growth between the high-performing brands in terms of word of mouth advocacy and low-performing brands is quite substantial. I think as more and more brands realize this, the more they will think about word of mouth as they're planning activities. And as they do, they will come to realize how big and influential it is.

Notes

Chapter 1

1. Neal Stewart, "PBR," NealStewart.com blog, accessed July 2014, http://nealstewart.com/case-studies/pbr-case-study/.
2. Beth Kowitt, "Let's Hear It for Hipster Beer," *CNN Money/Fortune*, December 2009, http://money.cnn.com/2009/12/10/news/companies /pbr_pabst_blue_ribbon.fortune/index.htm.
3. Ibid.
4. Stewart, "PBR."
5. Ibid.
6. Statistics cited in "Word of Mouth and Brand Advocates Stats," Zuberance Resources, accessed July 2014, http://www.zuberance.com /resources/resourcesStats.php.
7. Bill Wyman, "Did *Thriller* Really Sell a Hundred Million Copies?" *New Yorker* blog, January 4, 2013, http://www.newyorker.com/online /blogs/culture/2013/01/did-michael-jacksons-thriller-really-sell -a-hundred-million-copies.html.

Chapter 2

1. Brewers Association website, http://www.brewersassociation.org /statistics/national-beer-sales-production-data/.

Chapter 4

1. General Charles C. Krulak, "The Strategic Corporal: Leadership in the Three Block War," *Marines Magazine*, January 1999, http://www.au.af .mil/au/awc/awcgate/usmc/strategic_corporal.htm.
2. Ibid.

Chapter 5

1. International News Media Association (INMA), "Word of Mouth Plays Quantifiable Role in Driving Sales," June 2011, http://www.inma .org/article/index.cfm/46595-word of mouth-plays-quantifiable -role-in-driving-sales.

Chapter 7

1. Nicole Carter, "The Fascinating Psychology Behind Word-of-Mouth Marketing," *Inc.*, March 8, 2014, http://www.inc.com/nicole-carter /jonah-berger-marketing-word-of-mouth.html.
2. Carin Oliver, "Groundbreaking Survey Reveals How Diners Choose Restaurants," Angelsmith.net, August 7, 2012, http://angelsmith.net /inbound-marketing/groundbreaking-survey-reveals-how-diners -choose-restaurants/.
3. Meghan Casserly, "The Troubling Success of Tito's Handmade Vodka," *Forbes*, July 15, 2013, http://www.forbes.com/sites/meghan casserly/2013/06/26/haunted-spirits-the-troubling-success-of-titos -handmade-vodka/.
4. *Wikipedia*, "Tito's Vodka," accessed September 2014, http://en .wikipedia.org/wiki/Tito%27s_Vodka.

Chapter 8

1. Ed Keller and Brad Fay, Column: "Facebook Can't Replace Face-to-Face Conversation," *USA TODAY*, April 29, 2012, http://usatoday30 .usatoday.com/news/opinion/forum/story/2012-04-29/facebook -face-to-face/54629816/1.

Chapter 9

1. Jason R. Karp, Jeanne D. Johnston, Sandra Tecklenburg, Timothy D. Mickleborough, Alyce D. Fly, and Joel M. Stager, "Chocolate Milk as a Post-Exercise Recovery Aid," *International Journal of Sport Nutrition and Exercise Metabolism*, vol. 16, February 2006, 78–91.

Index

About the Author

Ted Wright is a native of Atlanta. He holds degrees from Hampden-Sydney College and the University of Chicago. He married way above his station, and his son is, by nature, loving and smart. The author drives too fast and enjoys great bourbon, but never at the same time. He hopes that you really like his book because lots of people told him that he should write it.